FIFTY YEARS OF MIRACLES

Experiencing the SUPERnatural

A 30-Day Devotional

By Larry B. Pyle

This book is designed to serve as a daily devotional, with a miracle testimony for each day of the month. As you conclude each chapter, take a few moments to reflect on what you have read, pray and believe God for the miracles you need in your life.

Fifty years of Miracles - Experiencing the SUPERnatural

Produced under the auspices of Successful Living Concepts, Inc.

3384 Crow Mountain Road
Russellville, AR 72802

ACKNOWLEDGMENTS

To Georgiann, my faithful companion, lover, best friend, encourager, and co-worker for more than half a century;

To Dr. Ron Cottle, my friend and mentor, who encouraged me to keep on going when I wanted to quit, and has consistently poured into my life since 1990;

To Thomas Hale, my friend and coworker who has patiently and faithfully stood by my side with technical and spiritual support for more than four decades;

To Wayne Drain, my faithful friend, counselor, and encourager for almost four decades;

To our children, Chris, Steve, and Aimee, whom I've known since you were born! Each of you has made me proud and thankful for your love, encouragement and support;

And finally, and foremost, to my wonderful Friend, Lord and Savior, Jesus Christ for your Agape!

TABLE OF CONTENTS

FOREWARD

I am so glad Pastor Larry Pyle has written stories of miracles he has experienced for over 50 years! I have known my friend, Pastor Larry Pyle, for 40+ of those years. In that time, I have observed Larry to be a man of faith, a forward thinker, and a man with the adventurous heart of a pioneer. Our church had its roots in the Jesus Movement of the early 1970's on the Arkansas Tech University campus near the church where Larry was a Youth Pastor. It was a remarkable move of the Holy Spirit that touched many young people across our city, region, and the nation. Larry was one of the few area pastors who welcomed and reached out to help us. He was not just trying to win us into his youth group. Larry saw God moving among young people and did what he could to encourage us.

Through the years Larry and I have co-hosted events in our city that included "March for Jesus," unity gatherings that crossed denominations, and several significant revival meetings. We have seen the Holy Spirit move in supernatural ways on many occasions. Larry and his wife Georgiann paid a price for being open to new ideas, new moves of the Spirit, and cooperation with churches outside their own denomination. But they have also known the joy of experiencing salvations, miracles of healing, real unity with other believers, and other modern-day miracles.

Miracles are signs that point us to the truth about Jesus. And that is what Pastor Larry does through personal testimonies in his new book, *Fifty Years of Miracles.*

Philip Yancy writes, *"A sign is not the same thing as proof; a sign is merely a marker for someone who is looking in the right direction."*

Pastor Larry has been an example for me to stay open to the leading of the Holy Spirit and to believe that Jesus has empowered us to perform miracles today in His name.

Fifty Years of Miracles will inspire you that the miracles Jesus performed while on earth are meant to continue as a normal part of the day-to-day lives for disciples who still follow Jesus' lead today! The amazing thing in the stories of miracles Pastor Larry writes about is that they are true—every one of them. And Larry would be the first to tell you that miracles do not just happen for special saints on special days. God promises miracles are signs that will follow all believers, everyday— everywhere they go for the glory of God (Hebrews 2:4).

E. Wayne Drain

Founding Pastor of City Church,

Co-Author of "He Still Speaks", and President of

Wayne Drain Ministries

PREFACE

"We are not human beings having a spiritual experience; we are spiritual beings having a human experience."

Teilhard de Chardin, a French philosopher, paleontologist, and Jesuit priest is often credited as author of this quote. Although researchers have not found this quotation in his works, it is evident that most residents of Earth believe we live in dual worlds. Even those who claim no belief in God readily refer to a realm beyond this physical, visual world. Almost daily we read the reports of the death of a celebrity or close friend who has "died and gone to be among the angels and is now looking down on us." Further, it is not uncommon to hear someone who professes no belief in God, angels or demons, refer to an individual who is "battling their demons."

Those who are familiar with the Holy Bible, are likely aware there are no less than 163 miracles recorded in the Old and New Testaments. From the miracle of creation in first chapter of Genesis to the sun and moon standing still for Joshua (Joshua 10); to a donkey speaking with a voice; to bread from heaven (Exodus 16) and water from solid rock (Exodus 17), the Old Testament is rich with examples of miraculous divine intervention in the lives of mankind. Then, moving to the New Testament, we find more than eighty examples, from the miracle of the virgin birth, to the water to wine miracle in Cana (John 2); to the feeding of five thousand, walking on water (Matthew 15) and many more.

Almost two thousand years ago, the Apostle, Paul, wrote to Christ-followers in Corinth: *"So we're not giving up. How could we! Even though on the outside it often looks like things are falling apart on us, on the inside, where God is making new life, not a day goes by without his unfolding grace. These hard times are small potatoes compared to the coming good times, the lavish celebration prepared for us. There's far more here than meets the eye. The things we see now are here today, gone tomorrow. But the things we can't see now will last forever"* (2 Corinthians 4:16-18 MSG).

The purpose of this book is to encourage readers to see beyond the visible realm and experience the presence, power and provision of Jehovah, the omnipresent, omniscient, omnipotent God, and allow Him to intervene and interact in your daily lives.

INTRODUCTION

At this writing, I have been in full time Gospel ministry for more than fifty years. Over these five decades I have personally witnessed and experienced situations and events that can only be described as miraculous. According to the *Merriam-Webster Dictionary*, a miracle is an extraordinary event manifesting divine intervention in human affairs. The *Oxford Dictionary* defines it as "a surprising and welcome event that is not explicable by natural or scientific laws and is therefore considered to be the work of a divine agency."

Obviously, there are those among us who deny the existence of God or deny His involvement in our Earthly journey, but naysayers have come too late to persuade me of their theories. As one writer put it, "We live on a blue planet that circles around a ball of fire next to a moon that moves the sea... and you don't believe in miracles?" (Anonymous). After more than five decades of experiencing the SUPERnatural, I have to agree with Ira Stanphill, who penned the words: "There are some things I may not know; there are some places I may not go; But this one thing I surely know; my God is real for I can feel Him in my soul."

DAY ONE:

RESTORED VOCAL CORDS

In the fall of 1965, at eighteen years old, I stepped onto the campus of Southwestern Assemblies of God College in Waxahachie, Texas and began preparing for my future. From my childhood I had been singing publicly and had been enrolled annually in the Stamps Baxter regional music schools. In my senior year of high school, I served as lead singer for a local quartet doing guest television appearances on KTAL in Texarkana, Arkansas and Shreveport, Louisiana. Therefore, it was only natural to join a vocal group on the college campus shortly after arriving. It didn't take long to form a group called "The Master's Four," consisting of Tim Dewey, singing baritone, Terry Clark, singing tenor, I was singing lead, and Charles Slagle was at the piano. A year later, Terry left the group and The Master's Four traveled on weekends and summer breaks representing SAGC and recruiting students. Cheryl Alderman married Tim Dewey and replaced Terry, and Alton Garrison replaced Charles at the piano. Without realizing it, the change in the makeup of the group placed me in a different vocal range, and the weekly singing schedule was taking a toll on my vocal chords without my knowledge. When I lost my voice and couldn't speak above a whisper, I thought I had a case of laryngitis. However, after three weeks of whispering, I attended a revival meeting in Fort Worth, conducted by the McDuff Brothers. That evening I visited with Roger McDuff, who had suffered and overcome several bouts with nodules on his vocal chords.

After Roger urged me to be examined by a Throat Specialist, my parents scheduled an appointment with a doctor in Texarkana. When the specialist examined me, he gave me a very disturbing report. He said, "Young man, you will never sing again, because your vocal chords are beyond repair... we cannot help you surgically." For someone who had been singing since childhood and aspiring to a singing career, this was a bombshell. I returned to college whispering and very discouraged. News of my condition soon spread throughout the campus and was soon shared with the student body in one of our morning chapel services. Our campus pastor shared my need with the students and asked the faculty and entire student body to believe God for a miracle. I was not immediately healed, but I awoke the next morning with a voice, and have been singing ever since, recording five solo albums in the process. Praise God that when earthly physicians have reached their limits, the Great Physician still heals! After fifty years of ministry, I am still singing and proclaiming the miraculous power of Jehovah Rapha!

Through the years as I have looked back on that crisis and victory in my life, it has strengthened my faith, knowing that Jesus Christ, not only paid for our spiritual healing, but our physical healing. Therefore, if this is a need in your life, my prayer for you is that your faith rises, and you are freed from every illness that has invaded your body. Remember, whatever crisis you are facing today, our Heavenly Father is greater than our problems or crises! Jeremiah 32:17 (NKJV), "Oh, Lord GOD! You have made the heavens and the earth by Your great power and outstretched arm. Nothing is too difficult for You!" Jeremiah 32:27 (NKJV), "Behold, I am the LORD, the God of all flesh. Is anything too difficult for Me?"

> *... He was pierced for our transgressions, he was*
> *crushed for our iniquities; the punishment that*
> *brought us peace was on him, and by his*
> *wounds we are healed.*
> *Isaiah 53:5 (NIV)*

Reflection

Dear friend, please recognize that TRUTH trumps FACTS! The physicians may present frightening facts and diagnoses, but our Savior, Redeemer and Healer, Jesus Christ said "I am the way the TRUTH and the life..." (John 14:6 NKJV). Today, apply the TRUTH to whatever discouraging FACTS you are facing and receive your victory in the name of Jesus!

DAY TWO:
MIRACLE MEAL

In December of 1969 I married a pastor's daughter in Laramie, Wyoming. Georgiann Clarke was the third of five children who grew up in the home of pioneer pastors, George and Faith Clarke. As church pioneers they experienced and witnessed the miracle-working power of God on many occasions. Georgiann recalls sitting down with her family at their dining table in Long Pine, Nebraska when she was five years old.

As the family gathered around the table, Dad Clarke said "Let's take time to thank God for our meal." But, Georgiann said, "Daddy, there IS no food to eat!" Dad Clarke replied, "But the Lord will provide!" Sure enough, as Dad Clarke completed this prayer of thanksgiving, there was a knock at their door. A lady, who they had never met, lived down the street from the

Clarkes, and was at the door with a casserole and a loaf of bread. When Mom Clarke opened the door, the neighbor said, "I know we have never met, but God spoke to me and impressed me to prepare a meal for you." After more than half a century Georgiann and I still praise the name and power of Jehovah Jireh, our provider!

Through five decades of marriage, there have been times when our outgo exceeded our income. However, through every season and every trial we have stood on the principle of tithing and giving to bless others, and our Heavenly Father has never failed to provide through unexpected sources.

Reflection

Do your needs today appear to be greater than your provision? Remember, you are a child of God. You have a Father in Heaven who knows the very hairs on your head and is mindful of your situation, and He sent His Son to redeem us from the bondage of Satan. Our Father is the same God who provided bread (manna) out of heaven and water out of rock for the

Children of Israel. He has not changed nor has His power diminished. The Apostle, Paul, wrote to the Philippian believers, *"I have all I need and more, now that I have received your gifts from Epaphroditus. They are a fragrant offering, an acceptable sacrifice, well-pleasing to God. **And my God will supply all your needs according to His glorious riches in Christ Jesus.**"* (Philippians 4:18-19).

Pray This Prayer with Me

"Father, I thank you that you love me and my family and watch over us to meet our every need. I thank you, that as I tithe and give to meet the needs of others you will supply ALL our needs according to your rich abundance in Christ Jesus. I now thank you in advance for your provision!"

DAY THREE:

TODDLER IN THE STREET

While serving as Youth Pastors at First Assembly of God in Russellville, Arkansas, Georgiann and I experienced an incredible act of God's mercy and protection. One balmy Wednesday night in 1973, following our youth service, Georgiann and I walked across the street to our home. After tucking our young sons in for the night, we turned out the lights and headed for bed. However, I was unable to sleep, feeling a terrible sense of foreboding. Unable to shake it, I shared it with Georgiann, and we both crawled out of bed, knelt on either side. Not knowing how or what to pray, for the next half hour, we prayed according to Romans 8:26-27, at times with groanings that could not be expressed with words. We spent the next half hour committing the situation to God. Approximately thirty minutes later, the heaviness lifted, and we crawled back into bed and slept soundly.

The next morning, we woke and began preparing for a busy day. According to our weekly schedule, our "quilting" ladies prepared a pot-luck lunch for our pastoral staff every Thursday, a block East of our home. After enjoying a delicious meal and great fellowship, I walked back home with the boys while Georgiann helped the ladies with the dishes. Arriving back at our house, I paused in the street to speak with our pastor and one of our elderly church members who was driving by and stopped for a brief conversation. Our boys, Chris and Steve, were busy playing on the sidewalk, with Chris pushing Steve along on a small plastic horse with wheels.

After conversing for several minutes, the elderly gentleman placed his large Chevy sedan in gear and started driving. A moment later, my heart almost stopped as I heard the sound of brakes screeching and a child screaming. I immediately looked toward the sidewalk where the boys had been playing. Only Chris was there, and I suddenly realized the screaming was coming from our four-year-old Steve underneath the big Chevrolet. With my heart pounding, I quickly ran down the street and crawled under the car, not knowing what I would find. There I found Steve, trapped under the front axle, still on the toy horse, but unable to move. With great care and determination, I maneuvered Steve's body until I could free him. Then, crawling from beneath the car, I stood him on his feet to determine if he could stand... he could!

I then examined him for lacerations and noted he was not bleeding, but was black, from head to toe, with asphalt from the street and grease from the automobile undercarriage. By that time, Georgiann had arrived, and we quickly placed Steve in our car and headed to the Emergency Room at St. Mary's Hospital. There, Steve was X-rayed and was thoroughly examined by Dr. Kenneth New, who informed us that Steve had suffered no fractures, nor lacerations, but did have a few bumps on his head, and his blond hair was blackened from the asphalt and grease. Now, here's rest of the story:

The night before the accident, Georgiann and I had been forewarned of pending danger. Not knowing how or what to pray we prayed according to Scriptures, then placed it in God's hands. The following morning, Georgiann dressed Chris in shorts, and a sleeveless shirt. Then, strangely, she dressed Steve in long jeans and a long-sleeved turtleneck sweatshirt... in spite of the fact that it was a humid July day. After our visit to the Emergency Room, it was evident the long pants and long sleeves had protected Steve from the road rash he would have suffered.

But here's an even stronger revelation, we came to realize: It became evident to us that our archenemy, Satan, intended to attack our family and kill our youngest son. However, one of the names of our God is Jehovah Jireh, which means "Our provider." Our English word, "Provider" is derived from Latin, "Pro-before" and "video-to see."

Therefore, the night before the accident, our God, Jehovah Jireh who sees our lives from beginning to end and beyond, not only saw a four-year old boy, but saw his future and his purpose in life, and prevented the enemy from destroying him.

According to God's plan, that little boy would grow up to succeed me as lead pastor of Life Center Church in the same city where Satan attempted to take his life. Then following me in the role of lead pastor, he would lead the church to expansion into two neighboring cities, with a combined Sunday attendance of more than 1500 seekers. We are thankful that Jehovah Jireh sees what lies ahead and provides a solution before we realize we have a need!

Reflection

As you reflect on the testimony you have just read, remember that Jehovah Jireh is your Father who knows your every need and sees what you are facing before you realize it, and has already set in motion the remedy for your situation. Remember that, although you may not even know how to pray about your situation, He has sent the Holy Spirit to assist you.

In Romans 8:26 Paul wrote that when we don't know how to pray, the Spirit helps our weakness and intercedes for us. The Greek word for "helps" is "*sunantilambanomo*" which means "together with against"! In other words, when we are at our weakest and don't know what we are facing or how to proceed, the Holy Spirit comes together with us against our enemy and intercedes for us for the victory! Read Romans 8:26-27, pray it over your situation and believe God for your answer today!

DAY FOUR:
HOME LOAN CLEARED

In 1977 we rented a larger house from Zora Miller, one of our board members at Life Center in Lakewood, California. We loved the home, and after living there several months, Zora offered to sell it to us. The thought of owning our own home there was very exciting. However, we had no idea how we could afford the down payment. We prayed about it, then committed it to the Lord to see if it was His will for us. A few days later, Otis McClendon, another of our deacons, approached us and offered to loan us $10,000 for the down payment. We were so grateful for the assistance by the McClendons, not realizing our Heavenly Father was about to teach us a power lesson on His economic principles. Approximately a year after we purchased the home, our church had outgrown our facilities and we launched a building program to construct a new worship center. At that time, as a young pastor, I knew far too little about the nature and ways of Jehovah Jireh, but Father was beginning to miraculously school us!

Following the directives from God and the counsel of our church board, I began to challenge the congregation to join me and Georgiann in regular sacrificial giving, above and beyond our tithe. Georgiann and I began to learn that the more we gave to help others and to expand the Kingdom of God, the more Abba poured back into our lives, and the promises given in Luke 6:38 became more than words spoken by Jesus 2000 years ago.

In a message to His followers, Jesus promised, *"Give, and it will be given to you. They will pour into your lap a good measure—pressed down, shaken together, and running over [with no space left for more]. For with the standard of measurement you use [when you do good to others], it will be measured to you in return"* (AMP).

On one occasion, Georgiann and I endorsed our entire weekly paycheck and placed it in our building fund, only to have our car break down the following week, costing us the exact amount we had given. When this occurred, I began to experience the tauntings of our spiritual accuser, challenging God's Word. In fact, the accuser impressed me that the next time we gave sacrificially he would hit us twice as hard. By the time our next building fund offering rolled around, Georgiann and I had just recovered from the loss we experienced with our car repairs. As Sunday approached, we prayed and asked Abba how much we should give in the offering. As we prayed our faith was strengthened and we decided to take a leap of faith and, again sow our entire paycheck into the building to show the enemy our trust in Abba was stronger than our fear of him.

That Sunday morning, during our first service I noticed a commotion in the back of the room, and saw my father-in-law, George Clarke, abruptly leave the building. At the conclusion of the service, I was shocked to hear that Otis McClendon had experienced a massive heart attack and died in his sleep. Otis, who was a member of our church board, a genuine servant of God and was the friend who loaned us the down payment on our house two years earlier. Approximately a month later, Otis' widow, Christine, pulled me and Georgiann aside after a Sunday service and informed us that Otis had instructed in his will that the balance of our loan (nearly $8000) was to be cleared at his passing. Georgiann and I had sown our entire paycheck into the morning offering, after the thief/accuser had stolen from us, and Jehovah Jireh had *"poured into our laps, good measure— pressed down, shaken together, and running over..."*

Reflection

The encouragement we trust you find in this chapter is the fact that we can't outgive God and His promises to us are true! In the sixth chapter of Matthew Jesus declares:

> *31 "Therefore do not worry, saying, 'What shall we eat?' or 'What shall we drink?' or 'What shall we wear?' 32 For after all these things the Gentiles seek. For your heavenly Father knows that you need all these things. 33 But seek first the kingdom of God and His righteousness, and*

all these things shall be added to you."

Matthew 6:31-33 (NKJV)

And Luke 6:38 tells us, *"Give, and it will be given to you. A good measure, pressed down, shaken together and running over, will be poured into your lap. For with the measure you use, it will be measured to you"* (NIV).

Pray This Prayer

"Father, I thank you that, in all circumstances and at all times you are my source of provision. I will continue to seek first your dominion in all my life, and I thank you today that you will provide more than enough for me and my family, so we will have an abundance to meet the needs of others!"

DAY FIVE:
MIRACLE SUNDAY

Back in the Seventies and Eighties, we were serving as lead pastors for Life Center Assembly of God in Lakewood, California, a suburb South of Los Angeles. By the mid-Seventies, our congregation had grown from 100 to more than 200 and we were desperate for a larger facility. As we surveyed the area around us, we discovered that available building lots were priced at more than a million dollars per acre, so we began to search out financing to construct a larger worship center on our site. While visiting one day with the president of Farmers & Merchants Bank in Lakewood, I presented our need for $350,000 to construct our new facility. It didn't take long for our bank president to inform me the loan was not feasible due to the fact that our congregation could not service a mortgage payment at 22.5% interest. (Yes, that was the interest rate during the Jimmy Carter Administration) Although we were disappointed, we realized that Father God must have a better plan, so we began praying for His plan and provision.

Not long after visiting with our bank president, some friends presented us with airline tickets to a pastors' conference in New Orleans, where each year, Pastor Charles Green hosted pastors from around the nation for a time of relaxation, restoration, and revelation. On the first night of the conference, Georgiann and I were seated among hundreds of pastors when the keynote speaker stopped in mid-sermon and said, "Will the pastor and wife from Lakewood, California please stand?" (Previously all the out of state pastors had shared our names and ministry locations) As we stood, the speaker, Pastor David Schoch, from Long Beach, said, "Pastor from Lakewood, though we pastor just a few miles apart, God has brought you 1500 miles for our paths to cross and for me to inform you God says, 'Do not lean to the arm of flesh, but do what God has called you to do!'" Although we were surprised, we didn't fully understand what had just happened in that church meeting, but we were about to discover the answer.

Arriving back at our hotel room following the message from Pastor Schoch, while Georgiann and I were preparing to retire for the evening, I turned on the television set and heard Evangelist Oral Roberts delivering a message. In the course of his message, Oral Roberts, said, "I have never started a new building with money. I always start with a hole in the ground."

Then it hit me, and the pieces of the puzzle began to fall into place. The plans we had drawn for our new worship center called for a basement. I immediately picked up the phone and called one of our board members in California and said, "Tell the other guys, we are starting our new building when we return. Although we didn't have the $25,000 needed for the basement, I knew we had heard phase One of God's plan.

Arriving back in Lakewood following the conference in New Orleans, we were excited about our building plans but aware we needed $25,000! Sitting in my office one morning I read a story of a congregation in Sherman, Texas that had raised thousands of dollars by reversing their tithes one Sunday, giving 90% instead of 10%. As I read it, I was strongly impressed to announce a Miracle Sunday on Thanksgiving Sunday, just ninety days away. The idea was to challenge our congregation to give 90% of our week's earnings on Thanksgiving Sunday and believe God to perform miracles with the remaining 10%. When I informed Father God that I was young and serving in my first pastorate, He didn't seem to share my anxiety!

On a Sunday morning three months before Thanksgiving, I made the announcement and presented the challenge. I shared the report from our bank president, denying us a mortgage loan and shared the prophetic message we had received in New Orleans. Then, I shared my belief that Jehovah Jireh wanted to show us His miracle power. So, everyone who wanted to take a daring step of faith was challenged to join me and Georgiann Miracle Sunday by reversing our tithe, giving 90% and trusting God to do miracles with the remaining 10%.

On the Sunday preceding Thanksgiving, I stepped to the pulpit to share a message on believing God for miracles. I knew God had spoken to me with the Miracle Sunday challenge, but still was anxious about sharing the message. At the end of my message, we received the offering. We needed $25,000 to launch the construction project. The ushers quickly counted the offering and brought me the total of $27,050.

The weeks following our initial Miracle Sunday were absolutely incredible as testimonies began to pour in. Our church members began to receive unexpected refunds from Utility companies; several received promotions and salary increases; some without work found employment; runaway teenagers came home; runaway spouses came home, and marriages were healed!

The testimonies following that first Miracle Sunday prompted many of our members to request another Miracle Sunday event. So, we did it again... and again, until eighteen months after we broke ground, we gathered in our brand new, debt-free auditorium.

In the final weeks of our fund-raising, the Anaheim Angels Baseball Team were on a winning streak and, as they pursued a major championship title, they adopted and publicized a theme, "YES WE CAN!" Capturing that theme, I had the same banner printed and hung it from the ceiling over our platform in our small auditorium. Each week as we gathered to pray and worship, our faith grew as we saw that banner proclaiming "YES, WE CAN!" But what our members didn't know was the fact that the word "CAN" was removable, and under it was the word "DID!"

Planted indelibly in my mind is the Sunday night we gathered to announce the totals of our final fund-raising efforts to complete the final phase of our new facility. Our small auditorium was packed that night with slightly more than one hundred people, anxiously waiting to hear the praise report. However, when we totaled our offerings for the day, to my disappointment, we were less than $500 from our goal. When I announced that to the congregation that night, a teenager said, "Pastor, I'll give $50 if I don't have to make my bed for the next month!" Her mother then raised her hand and said, "I'll give $100 if she WILL make her bed for the next month!" Then Mike Gurzi Jr, one of our young men, stood and said, "Pastor, I have a check for $250 coming from the Air Force. I'll endorse it to the church." For several minutes this continued till the balance of our goal was reached, and I reached up and ripped off the banner cover, causing the entire congregation to erupt in shouts of praise as they read, YES, WE DID!" It was obvious to us all that Jehovah Jireh still provides!

Reflection

The experience of meeting our financial goal that night in California strengthened our faith to believe our Father for even greater things, and He has never failed to do *"above and beyond what we can ask or think"* (Ephesians 3:20). What is the need or challenge facing you today? Read that promise again from Paul to the Ephesian believers! Our Father is pleased to exceed our request and our expectations according to the power at work WITHIN US!

Did you catch that? The potential to meet our needs is by the power of the Holy Spirit that dwells in us as believers and children of the King who desires to give us His Kingdom! Believe His Word today and exercise the *DUNAMIS* within you!

DAY SIX:
ANGEL AT OUR DOOR

One year, a few days after Thanksgiving, our car broke down and the repairs were the exact amount we had given in the Miracle Sunday offering. By the time we had recovered from the car repair expenses, we were preparing for another Miracle Sunday offering, and the devil began to taunt me with threats. He reminded me of our financial loss following the last Miracle Sunday and predicted another financial challenge would be a colossal failure.

Georigann's parents were staying in our home while on furlough from a mission field. One night, while Georgiann and I were gone to a meeting, a stranger knocked at our front door. Mom Clark was working at the kitchen sink and could see the stranger standing at the front door. She was so startled by the man's size, that she asked Dad Clarke to go to the door. Opening the door, Dad Clarke asked, "May I help you?" The stranger replied, "Is Pastor Pyle here?" When Dad Clarke informed him I was gone for the evening, the stranger said, "Please give him this money and tell him it's for him personally." Dad Clarke then asked, "Who shall I say brought the money?" "Tell him it's from the Lord" the man replied, then stepped into the darkness and disappeared, with no sign of any sort of vehicle.

When Georgiann and I returned home, Dad Clarke handed us three One Hundred Dollar bills and related the story of the stranger at the door. In our curiosity, we began to determine the identity of the stranger. Mom Clarke said the man was bald, very tall and muscular, wearing a white shirt, white pants and white shoes. "In fact," she said, "He looked just like Mr. Clean!"

Georgiann and I looked at the Hundred Dollar Bills that appeared so crisp and new, they looked like they had never been in circulation. We had no idea who had brought the money, nor why it was delivered, so we placed the money in a drawer and waited for an answer. The answer wasn't long coming. Three days later, we received a notice from our bank that we had overdrawn our checking account. Georgian had written a check for our car payment. Not realizing she had submitted the payment, I wrote a check for the same amount and mailed it, overdrawing your account by... you guessed it... three hundred dollars!

When I discovered this, I felt impressed by the Lord, "If I care enough about a three-hundred-dollar mistake in your checking account, I can take care of a three thousand dollar need, a thirty thousand dollar need or a three hundred thousand dollar need." I knew at the moment, everything we needed for the construction, or our new worship enter would be provided.

A few days after the stranger delivered the money, I was a guest on Channel 40 (Now Trinity Broadcasting Network) in Santa Ana. On the program that night, I shared the story of the stranger at the door. I looked into the camera and said to the viewing audience, "If you were the stranger at our door, please call in and let us know. Otherwise, I will believe an angel came to our door and delivered three hundred dollars!" No one called in, but a few days later, I received an amazing testimony.

One of the ladies from our church in California traveled to Oklahoma on vacation. While there she attended services in the church where she had grown up. Arriving back in California a few days later, she could hardly wait to see me on Sunday. Immediately following our Sunday morning service, she came running to me to share the excitement of what had occurred in Oklahoma.

As the Oklahoma pastor gave the invitation at the close of his message on Sunday evening, a first-time visitor responded and gave his heart to the Lord. The pastor then asked the man what brought him to the service. The visitor explained that he was an agnostic but had come to the service in desperation. Upon arrival at the service he said to God, "If you really exist, show me something supernatural here tonight." Then he said something very strange happened. He said that while the pastor was delivering his sermon, a man joined the pastor on the platform and began whispering to him.

The pastor stopped the visitor in mid-sentence, insisting no one had been on the platform with him that evening. "Oh yes," said the visitor, "a big man was there with you on the platform. Every time you stopped speaking for a moment, he whispered in your ear. Then you described everything I've been thinking; you even used some of the same words I've spoken today."

Still insisting he was alone on the platform, the pastor then asked the man to describe the man he saw. The visitor immediately responded: "He was a very large and muscular man with broad shoulders and a bald head. He was wearing a white shirt, white pants, and white shoes. In fact, preacher, he looked just like Mr. Clean!"

Now, fast forward fifteen hundred miles and a few years later. We had moved from Southern California to Russellville, Arkansas when I responded to a lady advertising some fence materials in a local newspaper. Arriving at her home, I rang her doorbell and was greeted by "Hello, Pastor Pyle!" I was shocked to see a widowed pastor's wife I had known for many years, so we spent several minutes catching up. She shared with me the loss of her husband then said, "Let me tell you how God comforted me the day he died!"

"The afternoon he died, I went to the hospital and was walking toward the ICU when a very tall, broad-shouldered man stopped me in the hallway. Although he was a stranger, he had the kindest voice and the softest blue eyes, I had ever seen. He told me he had been sent to tell me not to worry about my husband, 'we are taking care of him!'" Then she said to me, "Pastor Pyle, the strangest thing about this man was the way he was dressed. He was wearing white shoes, white pants, and shirt. He was bald and looked just like Mr. Clean on television!" I responded to her, "Sister, let me tell you about Mr. Clean!"

It's one thing to read of angelic visitations in the Scriptures, but it's quite another to believe angels are actually among us today. The writer to the Hebrews called them *"ministering spirits sent forth to serve the heirs of salvation"* (see Hebrews 1:14). You see friend, God loves you and me so much He has assigned His angels to serve us on our journey through this life. He wants to provide for us as His Covenant children. He may do that through very natural means, such as the job He has provided for us. But sometimes He chooses to provide for us by supernatural means. Don't forget He has been known to pay taxes with money taken from the mouth of a fish. Therefore, I'm persuaded He is more than willing to dispatch angels to our door, or to our sides, to remind us of His loving provision.

Reflection

Our Heavenly Father delights to minister to the needs of His children, and to reveal His love for us, He will often dispatch supernatural beings to come to our aid and provide for us in manners and measures beyond our physical and natural abilities. He wants to reveal His love for you in your present situation. Ask Him to move in your present position and circumstance in a way that will build your faith, and that of your family members and friends!

DAY SEVEN:
MIRACLE ON INTERSTATE 40

In May of 2008, Georgiann and I took a road trip back to Southern California to retrieve a cargo trailer we had left there the previous year. A few miles West of Oklahoma City, I became sleepy and stopped on the shoulder of the freeway for Georgiann to relieve me at the wheel. The following afternoon we arrived at the home of our friends, Bob and Nancy Stallings in Rossmoor, California.

After dinner and a great time of fellowship, we were preparing to retire for the evening, when I reached for my briefcase to retrieve an extremely confidential file I brought with me. To my horror, the file was missing. The missing file was of such confidentiality, and was so highly regulated, my license as a financial consultant could have been in jeopardy if I lost it. In my frustration, and in vain, I went back to our vehicle and turned it inside out searching for the file. Returning to our bedroom, I discussed my dilemma with Georgiann, and we decided to pray about it. As we prayed, we rehearsed Hebrews 1:14 (NIV) where we are reminded *"Are not all angels ministering spirits sent to serve those who will inherit salvation?"* We asked our Heavenly Father to dispatch an angel to locate and retrieve the file for us. We then committed it to God and went to bed.

The following morning at 5:30 I was awakened by my cell phone ringing. As I sleepily answered the phone, the man on the other end asked, "Is this Larry Pyle?" When I responded, he said, "Mr. Pyle, I found some documents on the North side of Interstate 40 about 25 miles West of Oklahoma City. It was actually quite amazing... I wasn't even at an exit! I just stopped on the side of the freeway for a moment and saw the file. It's looks like a very important file, so if you will provide me with an address, I will FedEx it to you this morning." I thanked the stranger profusely and informed him how we had prayed the night before. The next day, FedEx delivered the file, but we knew who had really retrieved it. Our loving Heavenly Father had heard our prayer and had dispatched a ministering angel!

Reflection

You will note this is one of several testimonies of angelic assistance, because I believe our Father really wants to teach us to move beyond our physical and natural resources and believe His Word to reveal His love and support by Supernatural means.

Are you facing a difficult or "impossible" situation? Present it to our Father right now and expect an answer!

DAY EIGHT:
THE LOST BRACELET

In the early Eighties, Georgiann and I took a group of friends on a Holy Land Tour. Before leaving Israel, we visited several gift shops hoping to purchase a souvenir of our trip. In one of the shops, Georgiann found a silver and gold bracelet she loved and wanted to purchase. I pretended it was too expensive, then slipped around while she was distracted, purchased it, and placed it in my jacket pocket. When we arrived back in the states, I gave Georgiann the bracelet. She was ecstatic, and it became one of her most cherished pieces of jewelry. However, on a Christmas outing at Big Bear Resort, the bracelet disappeared, and Georgiann was heartbroken. A few days earlier, she had accidentally brushed her left hand against a brick wall causing her Marquise-cut diamond wedding band to explode internally, due to a carbon pocket. At the subsequent loss of her cherished bracelet, Georgiann began to pray and wonder if she had placed too much value on temporal treasures.

Not financially able to replace her diamond wedding ring at the time, we replaced the stone with a Cubic Zirconium until we could afford a real diamond, and we prayed that somehow her bracelet could be found and returned. For months we had searched every nook and cranny of our home and our automobile, to no avail.

Then one day, after returning from the grocery store, Georgiann was getting out of the car, when she noticed a flash of light. There in the floorboard of our car, in plain view, was her cherished bracelet. At that moment, she stopped, lifted her hands, and said, "Thank you Father, for sending an angel to return my bracelet!"

Each day I'm more convinced that our Father loves us so much, He cares, not just about our spiritual welfare, but really cares about every aspect of our lives. The Psalmist wrote in

Psalm 37:4 "Delight yourself in the Lord, and He will give you the desires of your heart" (NIV).

Reflection

Have you misplaced something you value, or has something been stolen from you? Remember your Father loves you and delights to give you the desires of your heart. Tell Him now what has been misplaced or stolen. Ask Him for angelic assistance and believe Him for the answer!

DAY NINE:
ANGELIC PROTECTION

It has been opined by many that I have caused numerous guardian angels to retire early, due to close calls and near misses that have required enough titanium pins and screws in my body to start my own hardware store. My first memory of divine protection was an incident when I was a young teenager. Growing up in Southern Arkansas, our primary swimming hole (and baptismal tank) was a gravel pit a couple miles from our home. Although my mom had insisted I "stay away from the water hole till I learned to swim," I would often grab an inflated car tire tube and sneak off with some friends to the gravel pit. I will never forget the day I was floating in a tube when it overturned in the water, leaving me trapped upside down. Unable to free myself and unable to breathe, I began to panic and frantically paddle with my hands underneath the water. Just when it seemed I could hold my breath no longer, the tube floated to the shallow edge of the water, and I was able to flip it upright. Whether or not I've been accident prone, it seems evident God Almighty had a plan for my life that the thief (John 10:10) could not prevent because I had a mother who prayed over my life daily.

Many decades after the gravel pit incident, I gathered with my own wife and children to celebrate Christmas. Early on Christmas morning in 1989, our family gathered around our Christmas tree to open gifts. As the last gift was opened, I began gathering the wrapping paper and boxes, taking them to the garage just outside the door to our den. Stepping back into the house, I joined the family for breakfast. As we sat eating breakfast and enjoying a great time of fellowship, we heard a crackling sound coming from the garage. I quickly ran through our den into the laundry room, where I saw smoke coming in and around the door to the garage. When I opened the door, I felt the blast of heat from the fire. The day before, on Christmas Eve, I had cleaned the ashes from our fireplace and placed them into a metal bucket in the garage, unfortunately below a hanging rack of hunting clothing. Apparently, the ashes in the bucket also contained some live coals and had garnered enough oxygen to ignite both the coals and the clothing above the bucket. I quickly shut the door to the garage, but not before the house filled with smoke.

As I called 911, Georgiann and our children quickly began to gather our pets and run outside. I then grabbed a garden hose in an attempt to extinguish the flames. Unfortunately, our car was parked between me and the flames quickly crawling up the wall separating the garage from our laundry room and den. In an attempt to get to the water to the flames, I slid under the car from the rear bumper and began shooting water from underneath the car, not realizing the flames were melting the paint on the right rear panel. By the time the crew from our Fire Department arrived to finish extinguishing the flames the fire had severely damaged the garage interior and every room of our house was filled with smoke.

When the flames were finally extinguished, I backed our car out of the garage and examined it for damage. The flames had melted the paint on both sides of the gas tank filler. But there was no damage to the gas cap door. There was a space the size of a man's body, directly over the gas cap, but the gas cap area was untouched by the flames. Again, I believe a guardian angel was on duty!

Reflection

When was the last time your schedule was interrupted, or you were detoured from your intended route? Look back at that incident and remember Father directs our steps and our directions each day of our lives. Look back right now and examine those unexpected changes in your schedule or your route. Further, recall those situations in which you were in physical danger, but mysteriously or miraculously escaped.

As you do, I believe the Holy Spirit will bring to your memory someone you met or some message you received that will reveal Father's plan for your life on that occasion. Pause now and thank Him for directing your steps and providing you with divine connections and protections!

DAY TEN:
A THOUSAND-FOLD RETURN

Many years ago, while we were pastoring in Southern California, one of the ladies of our congregation in Lakewood brought me a check for two-hundred-dollars and suggested that we sow the money into the ministry of a neighboring pastor. She informed me the church was experiencing financial difficulty and the pastor had been forced to seek additional employment. Although I did not know the pastor personally, I was familiar with the location of his church building. Further, I was well acquainted with a number of our former members now attending his services one block away from our building. But something clicked in my spirit that day to respond to this opportunity to sow a financial seed. At three-thirty that afternoon I delivered a check from our treasury to the pastor around the corner.

FIFTY YEARS OF MIRACLES - EXPERIENCING THE *SUPER*NATURAL

The pastor had just arrived from his extra job when I met him in the parking lot of his church building. I introduced myself, informed him of our desire to sow into his ministry and handed him the check for two hundred dollars. As he received the check from me, he began to weep.

He said, "Brother, in all of my years of ministry here, no other pastor has ever sown into our ministry. I know you pastor the church around the corner from us, and I'm deeply moved that you would do this." With that he took my hand and prayed for me and our church. He prayed that God would multiply our seed back to us many times over what we had given.

Many months passed and I had forgotten the two hundred dollar seed we had sown into the neighboring church. I was very busy in my office the day my intercom rang, and the receptionist informed me that I had unscheduled visitors from out of town. With considerable reluctance I agreed to meet with the visitors for a few moments. Apologetically, they entered my office and began to renew our acquaintance and share their testimony. Five years earlier they had come forward for prayer in one of our services. While the dad was changing a flat tire beside the freeway, a moving van struck their car from behind, instantly killing their two teen-aged daughters and critically wounding the parents, who were both hospitalized for a year, and their medical bills amounted to hundreds of thousands of dollars. My heart was moved with compassion that day as I stood and prayed for a complete physical, emotional, and financial healing for that dear couple.

Now five years later, they returned to express their gratitude. They informed me that God had performed a miracle for them. A lengthy and difficult lawsuit had finally been settled and all of their medical bills had been paid. Then they informed me that they had already given a tithe to their home church in another city, but they had returned to thank and present me with a check for **two hundred thousand dollars** to help our church expand our facilities. My visitors had no idea that I had been petitioning God for a miracle of that same amount for our church, and I had no idea that God had responded to the prayer of a neighboring pastor over our two-hundred-dollar seed.

Reflection

Remember, we simply can't outgive God, and He delights to surprise us with His provision and His harvest as we are obedient to meet the needs of others. Open your heart today to His promptings. Do you know someone in need today? What can you do to meet that need? Remember, He loves to surprise us as we share His love and provisions with others! Ask Him today, to reveal the needs around you and then respond to His promptings!

DAY ELEVEN:

SOWING AND REAPING IN SPITE OF OUR NEED

While serving at Life Center in Lakewood, California, I was resting on a Sunday afternoon when I was notified of a crisis in a neighboring church in Riverside. Unfortunately, one of our sister churches was having their property mortgage foreclosed, while in the middle of their building program.

When I heard this, my heart was burdened for the congregation, and especially for the discouraged pastor. I knew on the following Sunday we needed to raise $25,000 to proceed with our next phase of construction. However, I felt compelled to put the crisis of our sister church ahead of our present need. So, during our Sunday evening service, I shared the Riverside crisis with our congregation, and we gave an impromptu offering to send to them. At the close of the service one of our ushers handed me a note. The offering we had given was $2,500. I immediately heard in my spirit, "You have given a tithe of your next building fund offering." The next day, our youth pastor and I delivered the check to the pastor in Riverside. He was so grateful and prayed with us for a bountiful harvest on the seed we had sown. The following Sunday, when we received the offering for our next phase of construction, it was slightly over $25,000! Jehovah Jireh was continuing to teach us the joy and the rewards of sowing and reaping!

Reflection

Writing to the believers in Phillipi, Paul thanked them for providing financial support for his ministry.

Philippians 4:14-19 (NIV):

> *14 ...It was good of you to share in my troubles.*
> *15 Moreover, as you Philippians know, in the*
> *early days of your acquaintance with the gospel,*
> *when I set out from Macedonia, not one church*
> *shared with me in the matter of giving and*

*receiving, except you only; 16 for even when I
was in Thessalonica, you sent me aid more than
once when I was in need. 17 Not that I desire
your gifts; what I desire is that more be credited
to your account. 18 I have received full payment
and have more than enough. I am amply
supplied, now that I have received from
Epaphroditus the gifts you sent. They are a
fragrant offering, an acceptable sacrifice,
pleasing to God. 19 **And my God will meet all
your needs** according to the riches of his glory
in Christ Jesus.*

Remember, God's Word is true, and He will provide for us in response to our providing for others! Keep sowing to bless others and expand His Kingdom and watch Him provide for your needs today!

DAY TWELVE:
THE CHEVY BLAZER

Duck season in Arkansas was just around the corner and I *needed* a truck. Not just any truck, but one with four-wheel drive. Recognizing my wife's inability to appreciate the value of such an investment (a common weakness among wives), I began shopping for a truck without her knowledge. Shortly, I found the truck I wanted in the classified ads of our local paper. I called the owner, left my office early and went to inspect the truck. It was just what I wanted, a four-wheel-drive Chevrolet S-10 Blazer. To my joy, the man accepted my offer which was five hundred dollars under wholesale value. I informed the man I would return the next day with the money for the vehicle. I drove home that evening bubbling with joy, assured that God had provided me with a wonderful blessing.

Over dinner, I broke the news to Georgiann. In great detail, I described the Blazer's paint job, interior, the four-wheel drive feature, but best of all, God's wonderful answer to my prayer. Silence gripped the dining room and a mysterious rush of cold air swept across my face as Georgiann abruptly stopped eating and looked at me in bewilderment. "You bought what?" she asked. "Larry, you know that we agreed not to make major purchases without first conferring with each other and praying together for God's wisdom."

Again, I explained to Georgiann how God had providentially led me to this vehicle five hundred dollars below wholesale. Furthermore, I informed her of my plan to sell our second car to provide money for the truck. She told me she wasn't impressed and that I had violated our agreement. Evidently, Georgiann did not see the spiritual element of my decision, so I quickly excused myself from the table and retired to my recliner to pout—I mean to ponder—the situation.

I knew Georgiann was right, and I had violated our agreement, but pride prevented me from admitting it readily.

Without her knowledge, I slipped into our bedroom and called the truck owner to tell him that I had broken my wife's trust and that I had decided not to purchase the vehicle. Amazingly, the man said, "No problem. Someone else is here wanting to buy the truck!" As I returned to my recliner, I tried to conceal my frustration, but the steam from my nose fogged my glasses.

The following day, as I returned home from my office, I stopped at a major intersection just in time to see the S-10 Blazer pass in front of me with its smiling new owner. I seethed as a little voice said, "You could have had that truck if not for your wife!" Not coincidentally, almost every day for a week, I saw the Blazer and its proud owner gliding down the street and preparing for duck season. Despite my spiritual superiority as the stronger vessel, I became morose and hardly talked with Georgiann for several days. Then came unexpected developments...

A phone call from one of our cell leaders informed me that a single mother in our church was unable to drive to work because her car's engine had broken down. Immediately, I heard a voice within me: "Give her your second car!" My thoughts immediately refocused on my plan to sell the car and to buy an all-terrain vehicle. However, I couldn't escape the impression to give away our car. Over dinner that evening, I mentioned the idea to Georgiann. She immediately responded, "That's God!" Sensing my need for a second opinion, I took the idea to our teen-aged daughter, Aimee. Her immediate response was "Great idea, Dad!"

The following day was the day after Thanksgiving, two days from duck season. Early in the morning, I phoned the single mother and verified her need for a vehicle. One hour later we delivered the car to her. When she asked the price of the car, I said, "Nothing, God said give it to you!" She was overjoyed and we were pleased with the opportunity to bless her. As we arrived home, the phone was ringing. The caller said, "Pastor Pyle, if you're still looking for a four-wheel drive, come and see me."

The caller was a used-car dealer in our city. Within thirty minutes I arrived at his dealership. He said to me, "I just got this SUV in and thought it might suit your needs... take it for a test drive." I drove the SUV all over town, then into the countryside, and back to the dealership. Interestingly, the vehicle was a blue four-wheel drive Chevrolet S-10 Blazer. Handing the keys back to the dealer, I asked Him, "How much are you asking for it?" He replied, "Nothing. God told me to give it to you!" God's Word is true, and his laws are immutable. They who sow will reap! (Luke 6:38)

Reflection

The provision of the vehicle for this single mother and the provision of the Chevy Blazer for me was a reminder of the message in Luke 6:38 (AMP):

> *Give, and it will be given to you. They will pour into your lap a good measure—pressed down, shaken together, and running over [with no space left for more]. For with the standard of measurement you use [when you do good to others], it will be measured to you in return."*

It was also a reminder that we reap what we sow. We do not reap corn when we sow beans, nor do we reap apples when we plant peaches. We sowed a vehicle, and our Father provided a vehicle! What do you need today? Sow it into the life of someone who needs it and expect a harvest!

DAY THIRTEEN:
THE FIFTY DOLLAR DUCK

One Sunday morning in the early 1990's I concluded my message and gave the benediction. As I prepared to leave the platform, I noticed a family standing in the aisle to my right. The dad, mom and three children were standing in a circle. Dad had his wallet in his hand and was conversing with his family when the Holy Spirit informed me they had no money for lunch. I immediately felt that I was to give them all the money in my wallet. I stepped from the platform, approached the family, and handed the Dad all the cash in my wallet, which totaled fifty dollars.

As I walked away from the family, it seemed I heard a voice mocking me and reminding me why I had stashed the cash. It was duck season, and the following day, I had planned to take our two teen-aged sons hunting in another county, so I saved the cash for the trip. However, as I listened to the accuser reminding me of my stupidity in giving away all my cash, I heard another voice reminding me of King Solomon's words.

In Proverbs 19:17, Solomon wrote, *"He who has pity on the poor lends to the Lord, And He will pay back what he has given"* (NKJV).

The following morning before dawn, I, along with our sons, Chris and Steve and one of their high school buddies headed South to one of our favorite hunting spots in Yell County. As we arrived, I dropped the teenagers on the North side of the lake, and I headed to the southside and set up my decoys. No sooner had I set the decoys and returned to my blind, I heard the teenagers blasting away on the north side and saw a beautiful flock of Mallards heading my way. As the mallards set their wings and began to land among my decoys, I fired three shots and dropped three Mallards. With great delight, I stepped out of my blind to retrieve the ducks. Then, as I picked up the last drake I saw a flash of light, as the sun illuminated a silver band on the leg of one of the drakes. As I looked closer, I read the message engraved in the band: "$50 Reward."

Members of the U.S. Fish and Game Commission had banded that drake and were tracking its migratory route. To receive my reward all I had to do was call the number on the band and report the location of the kill.

As I returned to my duck blind, I began to ponder what had just occurred and realized I had just experienced an incredible miracle reward. Just one day prior, I handed a needy family fifty dollars to provide lunch for them, and one day later a duck had returned my money!

However, the fuller revelation was this: Weeks before I gave the money, a mallard drake was banned in one of our northern states and was released to make its journey South. As I pondered this, I realized how many states the duck had crossed, how many lakes, rivers, and hunters it had passed to get to me. No doubt dozens of hunters in neighboring states had fired at that mallard to no avail. Then, arriving in Yell County, Arkansas, it had to fly over three teenagers firing at everything short of a C130, but no one could take this Mallard down, for it was on a divine mission to validate Solomon's promise regarding the rewards of giving to the poor!

Reflection

Through the years following the duck hunting experience, Georgiann and I have come to recognize and appreciate the fact one of our Father's names is Jehovah Jireh, "God who provides." It is a wonderful revelation that our Father not only knows our needs but makes provision for us before we realize we have a need!

Remember, **provision** comes from Latin Pro-before and Video-to-see! Therefore, He has already made provision for the needs in your life right now. So, go ahead and give Him praise for the blessing that is coming your way.

DAY FOURTEEN:
THE INHERITANCE

In 2002, I resigned as Senior Pastor of Life Center Church in Russellville, Arkansas, and passed the baton to our second son, Steven. Twelve years after its founding, I felt our church had reached a point of comfort and apathy wherein we had lost our vision for reaching the lost in our area. After much prayer, I felt it was time to pass the torch to another generation who could more effectively reach their culture.

As Georgiann and I stepped out of the pastoral leadership roles, we did so as a major step of faith, without any natural promise of provision, but with confidence that Jehovah Jireh was our Provider.

A few weeks after resigning as Senior Pastor I received a call from a friend of mine who was executor of a widow's estate. He informed me that our ministry had been listed in her will and invited me and Georgiann to the reading of the will. The widow who had passed was a member of our church, and regrettably had become so grumpy in the last season of her life that many were reluctant to even visit her. I had known her and her husband for many years and when he passed, I took on the role of watching after her, visiting her weekly and assisting her in any way I could.

As a result, it was not uncommon for her to ask me to make repairs in her home or stand on a ladder cleaning her lights and ceiling fans. I did this, not expecting anything in return but because I genuinely loved her and felt compassion for her, with her husband gone and no relatives nearby. Therefore, I was shocked to hear we were named in her will.

When I invited Georgiann to accompany me to the reading of the will, she declined, so I went alone. As the executor read the will, I was shocked to hear that the first beneficiary mentioned was Larry Pyle Ministries for $10,000. I was further shocked to hear that our inheritance was the only one mentioned that was not subject to probate but was to be dispensed immediately.

Reflection

Georgiann and I have come to realize that our Father delights in surprising us with His blessings. If we as Earthly parents find pleasure in surprising our children with gifts, how much more does our Heavenly Father take delight in us?

Matthew 7:11 (NIV), Jesus tells us,

> *"If you, then, though you are evil, know how to*
> *give good gifts to your children, how much*
> *more will your Father in heaven give good gifts*
> *to those who ask him!"*

Take a few moments to thank your Father for, not only your daily provisions, but those unexpected blessings that bring Him pleasure!

DAY FIFTEEN:
THE TWELVE THOUSAND DOLLAR CHECK

It should be noted here, that, after leaving our salaried position as lead pastors, Georgiann and I continued to tithe and to sow into the lives of others and to other ministries we had been supporting.

Several months after leaving our pastoral position I was scheduled to travel to Romania to teach at the Christian Life School of Theology in Timisoara. As I sat in a terminal at DFW in Dallas awaiting my flight to New York, my cell phone rang. Georgiann was weeping as she informed me she didn't have enough money to pay the bills due while I was gone halfway around the world. I prayed with her and tried to encourage her that God would provide for our needs.

A few minutes later, as the announcement came to board the New York flight, my phone rang again. This time Georgiann was crying and laughing simultaneously. She had walked to our mailbox to retrieve our mail and had discovered a financial miracle. In the mail was a letter from a family who had been members of our church in Lakewood, California twenty years earlier. This family had come into a tremendous amount of money and had wanted to share their blessing with us. However, they didn't know how to reach us. For six months they had been trying to locate us. When they finally obtained our mailing address, they sent us a letter with a donation of $12,000 for our ministry.

Here's the miracle: If the family in California had located us six months earlier, we would have still been lead pastors for Life Center Church in Russellville, Arkansas, without the pressing financial need. Now, without a regular salary and benefits, we were trusting Jehovah Jireh, our provider, and He once again proved Himself faithful!

Reflection

Once again, Georgiann were thrilled to recognize the blessing of knowing Jehovah Jireh sees ahead and provides for us BEFORE we even recognize we have the need! Take time right now to give Him praise and honor for being your Jehovah Jireh!

DAY SIXTEEN:

A DRIVE-BY SHOOTING AND A SPILLED SALAD

One Sunday evening following our worship time at Life Center Church in Lakewood, California, Georgiann and I joined some friends at a restaurant in Cerritos. On the Fourth of July, the restaurant was crowded, and traffic was heavy, but we managed to get a table near a window facing South Street, just one block south of the 605 Freeway. At the table with us were Jerry and Sue Stone, along with our youth pastors, Mark and Lola Allen. Sitting in a highchair at the end of our table was our toddler daughter, Aimee.

As we sat, enjoying our fellowship and appetizers, Lola Allen suddenly spilled her salad into her lap. As we all laughed and ducked our heads looking at the spilled salad, we heard a loud bang and the window over our table shattered. A drive-by shooter had fired a weapon through the window facing South Street. As we ducked our heads, the bullet had passed through the window directly over our heads and lodged in the wall a few inches above and behind Aimee's head. We all thanked our heavenly Father for the angel who walked by and spilled the salad in Lola's lap!

Reflection

As Georgiann and I looked back on that frightening situation, we were reminded of the words of the psalmist who wrote in Psalm 91:10-11 (NIV):

> *10 No harm will overtake you,*
>
> *no disaster will come near your tent.*
>
> *11 For he will command his angels concerning*
>
> *you*
>
> *to guard you in all your ways.*

That promise is to you and yours today, my friend. Take time now to thank your Father for His watchful care over you and your family!

DAY SEVENTEEN:
LEFT FOOT MIRACLE

One morning in June 2013, I woke early to travel to Dallas with Earl Helton, a pastor-friend in Russellville, Arkansas. Stepping from our hallway into our garage, I neglected to turn on the garage light and missed two steps leading down into the garage. The pain in my left foot was severe and it felt like my knee was pressed into my left armpit. Earl arrived and, at 2 AM, we headed for Dallas. The pain in my foot became worse throughout the day, and over the next few weeks, it became difficult to walk.

Finally, after weeks of hobbling on crutches, I sought help from a local podiatrist who informed me I had severely damaged the nerves and ligaments in my left foot. He further informed me the damage to my foot required a very difficult and painful surgery to repair it. Upon receiving this report, I opted to continue using crutches and praying for healing.

For the next two years, I was on and off the crutches and had many people praying for me. Then in the fall of 2015 I injured the foot again. While ministering at a Tres Dias event in Fayetteville Arkansas, I concluded my message, then stepped outside to return to my room. As I crossed the campus and headed to my dorm, I walked into a dark area and stepped off a three-foot embankment and landed hard on the asphalt driveway below. I immediately dropped to my knees, then to my hands as the pain began to shoot through my foot.

The following Monday, we called a noted surgeon in Little Rock and scheduled an appointment. A few days later, the surgery was performed which included splitting and relocating my left heel and inserting screws to hold it together, then shortening and rerouting the damaged ligament.

Unfortunately, after months of rehab therapy and immobility, the nerve pain was a daily test of endurance, so I sought the assistance of a noted neurosurgeon who recommended regular injections of steroids. The steroid injections were so painful, the doctor's body-builder assistant had to hold me down on each occasion. Finally, when I informed the surgeon, I could no longer tolerate the injections, he told me the last resort to relieve the pain was to kill the nerves in my foot. Of course, the downside of that procedure would mean no feeling whatsoever, which could lead to unknown injuries.

In May of 2018 Georgiann and I were preparing for another ministry trip to England and Romania when we received an invitation to attend a church leaders gathering at City Church (Fellowship of Christians) in Russellville, Arkansas. We gladly accepted the invitation and joined approximately 70 other leaders from around our region for a time of prayer, worship, and prophetic ministry.

During one of the sessions, a brother from Kenya stood and announced that a brother in the audience had been suffering from severe pain in his left foot and God wanted to heal him that day. Due to the speaker's broken English, I did not understand what he said, so Georgiann nudged me and said, "That's you!" At that, I stood and walked to the front where several men gathered around me and prayed for me. I then returned to my seat without feeling any particular improvement. However, without my knowledge, I was on the verge of a miracle.

During our lunch break Georgiann and I were seated at a round table visiting with friends, when a precious lady with silver hair approached me and asked if she would pray for my foot. "Of course, please do", I responded. She then knelt at my feet, removed my left shoe, placed my foot in her hands, and as she rubbed my foot, she said, "Holy Spirit, what do you want to do?" Asking me if it felt any different, I responded, "I believe it does." She then prayed again and informed me my foot was healed. I thanked her and we blended back into the group with no contact with her again.

At the conclusion of the conference, we drove home with no further thought of my foot. The next two days, I worked outside, mowing, weed eating, and walking on uneven surfaces for hours. Following the second day of yard work I came into our house and reported to Georgiann that I had been pain-free for the past two days, following the prayer for my foot. A few days later we left for England and Romania. Over the next two weeks, I walked many miles, (without a brace or boot) through airport terminals, the streets of London and the countryside of Romania. And now, in 2020, I am still free of the nerve pain that had tormented me for so long. All praise and honor to Jehovah Rapha, our Healer!

Reflection

Seven centuries before Jesus came to Earth, Isaiah wrote, *"... he was pierced for our transgressions, he was crushed for our iniquities; the punishment that brought us peace was on him, and by his wounds we are healed"* (Isaiah 53:5 NIV). We know that Isaiah was prophesying the redemption of mankind through the sacrifice of Christ at Calvary. However, we are also aware that the healing He provided was holistic, covering body, soul, and spirit.

Mark 16:17-18 (NIV) tells us:

> *"And these signs will follow those who believe:*
> *In My name they will cast out demons; they will*
> *speak in new tongues; they will pick up snakes*
> *with their hands; and when they drink deadly*
> *poison, it will not hurt them at all;* **they will**
> **place their hands on sick people, and they will**
> **get well."**

Reflection

If there is a need for physical healing in your body today, thank our Father right now for the price Jesus paid for our complete healing. Lay your hand on the area of your body that suffers today and take authority over affliction in the powerful name of Jesus. Speak to any spirit of infirmity attacking your body today and command it to loose its hold in the name of Jesus, then thank our Father for total victory!

DAY EIGHTEEN:
CITY COUNCIL MIRACLE

Prayer Moves Mountains, Curtains, and City Councils!

Some of our neighbors were angry with us because our church had grown rapidly from one hundred in Sunday morning attendance to well over five hundred. Our little building was landlocked on less than an acre in a crowded suburb of Los Angeles, and with only thirty-two parking spaces, our attendees parked blocks away and were shuttled to our worship services. Not only were the neighbors angry, but so were the Southern California demons. Death threats against me and my family were common, from the homosexual community, from the "Lakewood Coven," and from the late-night callers claiming to be "Beelzebub," himself. So, when the night arrived for our meeting with the City Council, tension was high.

The Lakewood City Planning Commission had denied our request for a building permit to expand our worship center to accommodate more people, so we appealed their decision to the City Council. In the meantime, as the death threats increased, so did our intercessory prayer.

On the night of the City Council meeting, our prayer warriors arrived early and filled the council chambers, both physically and spiritually. Ours was obviously the hottest item on the agenda that evening, so our appeal was brought to the floor for debate quickly. Our opponents were ready for battle and began charging us with disturbing the peace and taking over their neighborhood. Then, a sequence of strange events began to unfold in the room.

A Catholic priest who had been waiting to address another issue that evening, suddenly stepped to the microphone and began to speak on our behalf. In very broken English he addressed the council members: "Ladies and Gentlemen, surely you wouldn't deny this church their building permit... surely not in America... surely not in America. If you deny this church their permit to build, your sons and daughters will die in the streets of this city... they will die by drugs, alcohol, and gunfire. This community needs this church... surely you will not deny them their permit!" With that the stranger sat down and one of our neighbors took his place at the microphone.

"Look closely at me," she said. "Please note that I'm standing on two feet. I have two legs and two feet because of that church and that pastor. Last year I had an accident, and my right leg was seriously injured and developed advanced gangrene. My family physician scheduled me for surgery to remove my leg, but one day that pastor came across the street and prayed for me... Look at me... I have two feet and two legs. I am completely healed. This community needs that church; please don't deny them their building permit!"

Late in the evening, after hearing many witnesses for and against our appeal, the city council prepared to vote. Then the unexpected and unexplainable happened! Suddenly the lights in the room began to blink off and on, and the electronic curtains behind the council members began to open and close repeatedly. This strange occurrence lasted several minutes as we all sat in astonishment.

When finally, the curtains stopped moving and the lights remained on, one of the council members spoke. He was the only Mormon on the city council, and I had wondered where he would stand on our appeal, so as he spoke, he had everyone's attention. "Mr. Chairman," he said, "It's obvious we are not in control of this meeting here tonight; there seems to be a higher power at work. I move that we grant this church their building permit unconditionally!"

Reflection

The miracle in the Lakewood City Council chambers that night has bolstered our faith many times over the decades since! Many times since then we have faced difficulties that only God could overcome. Each time we face insurmountable challenges we remember the promise our Father gave His children through Isaiah:

"No weapon forged against you will prevail,

and you will refute every tongue that accuses

you.

This is the heritage of the servants of the LORD,

and this is their vindication from me,"

declares the LORD.

Isaiah 54:17 NIV

What are you facing today? Although you may not have the answers to your questions, your Father knows and has placed His Spirit in you and will give you victory. Take time now to thank Him that victory is yours in Jesus' name!

DAY NINETEEN:
HAPPY BIRTHDAY, PASTOR!

Back in the 1990's, the men of our church prepared a construction project for an orphanage in Honduras. Along with the construction workers, several doctors and nurses joined the team to provide examinations and minor medical aid to the Honduran orphans. Our team flew out of Little Rock, Arkansas on Saturday, and I intended to join them on Sunday after our morning church meetings.

Following our Sunday morning service, Georgiann drove me to Little Rock where I boarded a flight for San Pedro Sula, Honduras, where I would be met by a Honduran church leader and driven to our mission site in the mountains several hours North. However, due to inclement weather, we were forced to land in a city several hours from our intended destination, creating quite a dilemma for me. Not only was I in the wrong city. I spoke no Spanish and had no idea how to contact my friends or my driver waiting for me in San Pedro.

Already weary from the weekend of ministry and the air travel, I sat on my luggage in the baggage area and prayed for God to provide me with wisdom and direction. As I sat there, I listened intently, desperately trying to locate someone speaking English. Then, to my amazement I noticed a young Honduran lady speaking perfect English to a group of tourists.

Quickly, I walked over to the group and explained my predicament. The young Honduran guide then very kindly volunteered to assist me with phone calls and arranged for me to purchase a ticket on a bus to San Pedro Sula. After waiting another ninety minutes, my bus arrived, and I quickly boarded and located an empty seat. Due to the fact our bus trip included numerous stops, unloading, and taking on new passengers, I was very pleasantly surprised when an American man in military uniform, boarded and sat beside me. He seemed equally pleased to find another American on board and, as we proceeded on our journey, he inquired where I was headed and the purpose of my journey. When I informed him I was joining a missions team at an orphanage in the mountains North of San Pedro Sula, he seemed very interested in our mission.

A couple hours into our journey, the military man informed me he was the senior commander of a U.S. Air Force Base there in Honduras. Then, as the bus approached his destination, he turned to me, handed me his card, and said, "Call me if you need anything and if you ever need a helicopter, let me know!" As he left the bus, I thanked him, and I thanked God for the obvious divine encounter.

At 10 PM, we arrived at the bus station on the outskirts of San Pedro Sula, and I was pleased to find a young Honduran pastor waiting to drive me into the mountains to meet our team. The following night, following a tiring day of assisting our team members, we gathered for a meal that included a surprise birthday party for the Honduran missionary pastor. As I sat and visited with the pastor, I discovered he had spent several years traveling from village to village through the mountains sharing the Gospel with all who would listen. His primary mode of transportation was an old motor bike that had finally died of old age and burnout.

When I discovered his motorbike was out of service and his travel to the remote villages was limited to hiking or riding a rusted bicycle, I said to the pastor, "What would you really like for your birthday?" I was astonished when he jokingly replied, "I would like to have a helicopter!" At that, I reached into my pocket and retrieved the card of the Military Commander. I handed the card to the pastor and said, "Happy birthday!"

Reflection

Looking back on that trip to Honduras has reminded me how our Father directs our steps and often changes our schedules or reroutes us in order to connect us with His preplanned appointments and connections.

Take a few moments to thank Him for directing your steps, your plans, and your decisions to perform His will and plans for your good and His glory! Then be willing and patient to know he has written every day of your life in His book before one of them

came to be (Psalm 139:16).

DAY TWENTY:
SOWING AND REAPING DURING A FAMINE

Over the past fifty years of church leadership, I've had the privilege of assisting many pastors in reducing and eliminating church debt. One month in the mid-nineties I was contacted by a pastor in Southern Florida who was desperate for help. His entire church campus had been destroyed by a powerful hurricane, and following their insurance settlement, they had rebuilt at a cost of several million dollars. Unfortunately, shortly after moving into their new facilities, their area suffered a significant financial downturn, and many of the church members were forced to move away to seek employment.

After visiting with the pastor, I agreed to travel to Florida, and I asked him to send me a copy of their last annual financial statement, along with a file of their financial statements over the past six months. I told him I would review and pray over the financial statements, then pray for wisdom to address their financial crisis.

Over the next few weeks, I contacted the pastor in Florida several times, reminding him to forward the financial reports. Each time, he said he would promptly mail the reports. Unfortunately, on the day I was scheduled to fly to Florida, I had not received a single report from the pastor, and therefore, had no knowledge of the predicament I was walking into.

As I boarded my flight from Little Rock to Miami, I took my seat and immediately began praying for God to give me knowledge and wisdom for the situation I was facing. As our plane reached its cruising altitude, I felt impressed to reach for my Bible and read the twenty-sixth chapter of Genesis. I was curiously anxious to read the passage and see what possible connection it would have with the Florida congregation I was trying to help.

Genesis 26 describes a famine in the land where Isaac was living. In verse three, the Lord said to Isaac, "2 ... Do not go down to Egypt; live in the land where I tell you to live. 3 Stay in this land for a while, and I will be with you and bless you... 12 Isaac planted crops in that land and in the same year reaped a hundredfold, because the Lord blessed him" (Genesis 2-3, 12 NIV).

As I read and pondered over the Genesis passage, I felt impressed to share it with the Florida congregation and encourage them, not to run, but to trust God and sow in their land of famine and believe God to miraculously provide for them. More than half of the congregation had left and many more were seriously considering moving away.

On Sunday morning when I was introduced, I stepped to the pulpit, ignorant of the severity of their financial situation, but I was totally confident that Jehovah Jireh knew the details and had a solution.

At the conclusion of my message from Genesis 26, I challenged the congregation to believe God for miracles and, in spite of their financial famine, to sow into their land by faith and watch God do miracles. I then asked the ushers to prepare to receive an offering for the church and I asked the congregation to stand and ask God what seed they should sow in their land of famine.

Then I felt impressed to share a Word of Knowledge (1 Corinthians 12:8). I said "As a sign of what God wants to do here, He's going to show you a miracle here this morning. There is a couple here who has been trying to collect a debt for several years and have recently given up on ever being repaid, but God is going to show you He is your provider!"

No sooner had the words left my lips when I saw a commotion in the rear of the auditorium. A gentleman walked into the auditorium and was speaking to an usher, looking for a certain couple. The usher pointed to the couple on the end of a pew. The man walked forward and stopped and began speaking to the couple, then began handing them cash. After the ushers collected the offering, and I was preparing to close the service, the couple approached by the latecomer, stepped to the front, and asked if they could share something.

As I held the microphone for them, the husband said the gentleman that approached them had owed them money for the past three years and had made no effort to pay them. Although they had prayed about the matter many times, they had given up hope of ever receiving payment. However, as they stood with the congregation and prayed, and prepared to place a check in the offering, the debtor approached them, apologized for taking so long, and proceeded to pay them in full with hundred-dollar bills. I, as well as the congregation, was reminded that Jehovah Jireh is never limited by our circumstances, and He still provides for those who trust Him and are willing to sow, even in a time of famine!

Reflection

Is there a famine in your life now? Perhaps you are going through a time of scarcity and lack, but don't stop sowing.

Over the past five decades of marriage and ministry, Georgiann and I have literally given our way out of financial crises. Our Father has never failed to provide above and beyond our needs as we have continued to tithe and give liberally, and He will do the same for you.

Take a few moments and thank Him for His provision. Ask Him to show you where you need to sow in your time of famine, then thank Him in advance for your harvest!

DAY TWENTY-ONE:
PHONE CALL FROM BEYOND THE GRAVE

Since 2005 I have served as a Police Chaplain, working with Law Enforcement agencies from coast to coast. In that capacity, I have witnessed more than my share of tragedies, including suicides, homicides, train and auto wrecks, tornadoes, and drownings. Due to the fact that most of the tragedies have involved strangers, I have been able to minister to family members and their friends without any personal emotional trauma. However, that all changed in October of 2015.

Georgiann and I were driving into town at 9 AM when I received a call, dispatching me to a suicide scene on the West side of Russellville, Arkansas. Arriving at the address, I parked a half block away to shield Georgiann from the scene. As I walked toward the entrance of the house, I noticed the County

Coroner was on the scene and I assumed the victim's body was covered. However, not only was the body uncovered, but it was also a close friend of mine and a former elder in our church. His body was slumped in a chair under the carport where he had ended his life with a 12-gauge shotgun. I will spare the reader the gory details.

However, suffice it to say, the scene would have been difficult for Hollywood horror flicks to replicate. Although God enabled me to minister to many hurting friends and neighbors in the memorial service, my years of training and experience were not adequate to take me through the PTSD I would encounter over the next twelve months. Thanks to my friends and colleagues at the Pope County Sheriff's Office and our dear friend and professional counselor, Melinda Taylor, I was able to cope with the flashbacks. However, one year later I was severely tested.

Almost one year to the date of my friend's suicide I was speaking for a Men's Tres Dias Weekend in Fayetteville, Arkansas. On the first night of the event, I concluded my talk and took my seat at a table with the camp directors.

Immediately as I took my seat my phone began to vibrate in my pocket. As I removed the phone to check the call, I noticed the call originated in Russellville, Arkansas, where I was on call 24-7.

Immediately, I stepped out a side door and returned the call. As the phone rang, I was astonished to see the name on the screen was that of my friend who had taken his life one year earlier. Of course, there was no answer, but I was shaken. Walking back into the conference room, I was so disturbed, I could hardly wait for the session to end. As the session closed, I immediately shared my experience with one of our prayer leaders. His response was both surprising and enlightening. He said, "Larry, why was your deceased friend's name still in your phone directory?" I replied, "Because I neglected to remove it!" He then reminded me of the words of Jesus recorded in John 14:30b "The ruler of this world is coming, but he has nothing in Me" (NKJV).

Then he informed me that any tragic event, any sin, or emotional trauma we experience, but do not commit to God for

His healing and removal, will remain available to Satan to retrieve, and use against us! Whether it's a divorce, sin of immorality, or tragedy in our lives, it must be submitted to God and removed from our memory directory. Right then and there my friend prayed with me, I deleted the name of my deceased friend from my phone directory, committed the memory to my Heavenly Father and have had no torment since.

Reflection

Is there something in your past that you have not deleted and submitted to your Father? Possibly it was a broken marriage and divorce... possibly the guilt of a sin that still torments you... or it may be a traumatic event that shattered your emotions.

Right now, in this moment, submit it to your Heavenly Father, then, in the name of Jesus, press the "delete" button and receive your deliverance and freedom! Take a few moments now and thank Him for your victory!

DAY TWENTY-TWO:
THE DYING SOCIALITE

The year was 1975 and Georgiann and I were serving in our first roles as lead pastors at First Assembly of God in Lakewood, California. During a Sunday morning gathering, shortly after we arrived in Lakewood, as I gave an invitation for salvation, an elderly gentleman, walking with a cane, came down the center aisle and surrendered his heart to the Lord. When the meeting concluded I discovered, not only was this his seventieth birthday, it was also his first time in a conservative evangelical church.

His name was Jack. He was one of the directors of the Los Angeles Athletic Club who had recently been diagnosed with a brain tumor and wanted to get to know God. Jack asked me if I would visit him in his home in Long Beach, and over the next twelve months, I did just that, visiting with him, reading, and explaining Scriptures and answering his questions as best I could. As the weeks and months progressed, so did his cancerous brain tumor, and the day came when he was admitted to the Long Beach Memorial Hospital where his life would end.

Early the next morning, one of Jack's daughters called me and I joined her, her sister and mother at Jack's bedside in the hospital. Jack had slipped into a coma, his eyes were fixed in an incognizant stare, and his attending physicians said his vital organs were shutting down and he would soon be gone. My office was located approximately ten miles from Long Beach Memorial, so throughout the day I stopped in to check on the family.

At eight PM, I walked into Jack's room again to visit with the family. His daughters were standing on the back side of his bed, and his wife and I stood on the other side visiting and watching the monitors above his head. At approximately 8:15 PM Jack suddenly sat straight up in his bed, took one long, last breath and slumped back onto his pillow. However, as he did, we witnessed a miracle. As his head hit his pillow, Jack turned his face toward me and his wife. Personality returned to his eyes as he smiled, winked, and slipped into eternity.

In more than fifty years of ministry, and having sat with countless dying patients, I have never witnessed anything like I saw that evening. For more than eight hours, Jack had been comatose with his eyes fixed with no expression or ability to communicate. However, as he drew his very last breath, Jack's loving Heavenly Father allowed his personality and consciousness to return just long enough to smile and wink at us, as if to say, "It is well with my soul!"

Reflection

Since that day in Long Beach Memorial Hospital, I have been convinced that our Father caused Jack's strength and consciousness to return long enough to reveal to his family his peace with God and his assurance of salvation and eternal life.

Take a moment now and ask our Father to reveal His power, His nature, and His glory in and through you and those you come in contact with today then thank Him in advance for divine encounters!

DAY TWENTY-THREE:
THE VODKA AND THE NEW WINE

In the early months of 1971, Georgiann and I moved from Glenwood, Minnesota to Fort Worth, Texas, where Challenge Ministries was relocated, to be more centrally located for our television production and travel. I had been serving as the crusade and television vocalist for Evangelist L. D. Kramer and Challenge Ministries, since 1969. Our son, Chris, was less than three months old when we moved into an apartment in Euless/Hurst, on the outskirts of Fort Worth. Georgiann was a stay-at-home mom, while I worked in the ministry headquarters, proofreading books for Evangelist Kramer, and helping produce our television programs during the week and traveling in crusades on weekends.

Not long after moving to Fort Worth, stress from my work schedule, parenting, and a tight financial budget began to wear on me and Georgiann to the point we reached a boiling point one day and engaged in a terrible argument.

Finally, in desperation, we both said, "I'm leaving," and headed for the door. Unfortunately for Georgiann, I had the keys to the car and escaped to the parking lot before she could gather up Chris and head for the door. I sped out of our parking lot and headed South on Interstate 20, not really knowing where I was going.

Then, I recalled my high school days, when my cousins and friends would drink alcohol when they wanted to escape reality and have a "good time." Having been raised in a strict Pentecostal home, I had never partaken of beer, wine, or liquor, but this day, I was curious enough to give it a try to drown my depression and anger. Driving South out of Metro Fort Worth, I noticed a sign for a liquor store, exited the freeway and drove to the store. I was extremely nervous as I entered the store, and totally caught off guard when the clerk said, "What can I get for you?" Not knowing the difference between beer, wine, or whiskey, the first word that came out of my mouth was "Vodka!"

When the clerk stuffed a pint of Vodka in a paper bag, I nervously paid him and headed for my car. At the moment, I was so depressed and angry at my young wife, I was determined to go home and get drunk in front of her.

When I arrived back at our apartment, I walked in, pulled the Vodka from the paper bag, and headed to our kitchen. With Georgiann watching me in total shock, I removed the cap from the bottle, and downed the whole pint. As I swallowed it, my throat burned like fire, but I was determined to show Georgiann, AND God, that I could escape reality and drown my sorrows!

Not until years later did I realize I could have died from alcohol poisoning, had my Heavenly Father not protected me from my ignorance! After emptying the bottle of Vodka, I walked into our living room, sat on our couch, and waited to get drunk. Instead, the Vodka didn't faze me at all. Strangely, I didn't get drunk nor sick. I only became angry that it didn't work for me.

Now, fast forward twenty-five years! In 1995 we were serving as lead pastors for Life Center Church in Russellville, Arkansas, when an incredible spiritual explosion hit our church. Georgiann and I had visited, and had been impacted, by the Rodney Howard Browne meetings, the Toronto and Pensacola outpourings, and were hungry for the Supernatural, when revival came to our church. One Saturday night, as I was leaving our prayer meeting, Georgiann called me and asked me to bring some ice cream to share with some friends who had stopped by our home.

Our young nephew, Ryan Clarke, was riding with me when we stopped at a grocery store for ice cream. Entering the store, we walked back to the frozen food section and located the brand we wanted. When I opened the freezer door and reached in, I felt like I was hit with a 2x4! Suddenly, I was so drunk, I could hardly stand. As I staggered, with slurred speech, I asked Ryan to help me walk.

Shocked and embarrassed by the situation, I prayed that the clerk at the cash register would not try to engage me in conversation. Trying to stay on my feet, I quickly placed the ice cream on the checkout stand, the clerk gave me the total and I paid her, without having to say a word. Quickly, but carefully, Ryan and I walked to our car.

Ryan and I got in the car, I started the engine, and just sat there for a moment, praying. Still dazed by the incident inside the store, I began to question God. "What just happened to me? Why here, and why now?" As soon as I asked, I heard an answer in my spirit. "Do you remember what happened in Fort Worth, Texas twenty-five years ago?" Immediately, I recalled the Vodka experiment, and my attempt to get drunk, as the Holy Spirit informed me, "I never allowed you to know the counterfeit, because I wanted you to know the REAL thing!"

I then realized my Heavenly Father had protected me from my ignorance, AND from the alcoholism on both sides of my family and had slammed me with the intoxicating power of the

Holy Spirit (Acts 2:13-15), that left no hangover or damage to my physical body!

However, it did leave me with an addiction! Since that experience, when I am exposed to, or engaged in deep praise and worship, I often become so intoxicated I can't stand or walk without staggering.

Case in point: A few years ago, Georgiann and I were invited to minister at an Assemblies of God Church in Highlands, Missouri. At the conclusion of my message, I invited those who wanted special prayer to join me at the front, where we began to lay hands on and pray with individuals with special needs. While the worship team ministered and I moved along the prayer line, the more I prayed, the more intoxicated I became to the point I could no longer stand, so I collapsed on the edge of the platform. The pastor noticed what had happened and thought I was sick, so he invited several men to gather around and pray for me. As I sat on the edge of the platform, totally intoxicated by the power of the Holy Spirit, the guys prayed for me, as Georgiann stood on the front row with her hand over her mouth, and camera in hand, recording the moment, and trying to conceal her laughter at the scene unfolding in front of her.

Reflection

Without a doubt, the pleasures of this world and its physical stimulants, can't compare with the New Wine of the Holy Spirit!

Ask Holy Spirit to fill you to overflowing today, so you may bask in His presence and experience the Joy of the Lord which provides our strength!

DAY TWENTY-FOUR:
THE "WIDOW MAKER"

In 2009, Georgiann began experiencing shortness of breath to the extent, she had difficulty walking to and from our mailbox, and could hardly dry her hair without shortness of breath.

After consulting our family physician, he recommended she travel to Little Rock for a Cardiogram and stress test. After leaving our physician's office we called our local, national, and international prayer partners to believe with us for her healing. We then called and scheduled the tests in Little Rock.

A few days later, we drove to Little Rock for the stress test and cardiogram, fully believing for a good report. After the staff applied the electrical receptors to her body, Georgiann stepped onto the treadmill and began walking. However, after only two minutes she became faint, and the nurses quickly removed her from the treadmill.

Coincidentally... NO, by God's providence, Dr. Andrew Henry, one of the top Cardiologists in our region, was walking through the hallway getting ready to leave for the airport for vacation. One of the nurses stopped him and asked him to look at Georgiann's cardiogram. With a quick review of her test, Dr. Henry said she required immediate surgery.

Unfortunately, the Operating Room was not immediately available at the Little Rock Heart Hospital, so Georgiann was quickly rushed across town to St. Vincent's Hospital, where Dr. Henry (who postponed his flight) performed the emergency procedure.

After calling our children, close friends, and intercessors, I sat alone in the waiting room, praying and believing for a good report. Eventually, the door opened, and Dr. Henry came to my side and said, "Well, pastor, I saved your wife's life today! Her largest artery, called the "Widow Maker" was 95% blocked and we installed a stent to save her life. You may take her home after she is awake and dressed."

I expressed my deep gratitude to Dr. Henry, then reminded him of the words of the Psalmist who wrote *"The steps of a good man are ordered by the LORD, And he delights in his way. Though he fall, he shall not be utterly cast down; For the LORD upholds him with his hand"* (Psalm 37:23-24 NKJV). I then had the privilege of praying with and for Dr. Henry for God's blessing in and over his life. A few months later, Dr. Henry was very seriously injured in a motorcycle accident that could have been fatal, BUT GOD!

Because He knows us so intimately, He numbers the hairs on our heads, and He knows what we need before we are aware of the need. We had no idea Georgiann's life was in extreme danger with the blocked artery, and Dr. Henry had no idea his schedule would be interrupted that day, BUT GOD!

Reflection

Dear reader, whatever your situation or your crisis today, know that your heavenly Father, not only orders your steps, but wrote the days of your life in His book before one of them came to be (Psalm 139) and, through the sacrifice of His Son, has made provision for your body, soul, and spirit!

DAY TWENTY-FIVE:
THE AUTO-ELECTRICAL PROBLEM

Not long ago after a local hunting trip, I noticed the interior lights on my Jeep Cherokee would not shut off. I knew, if left on, the lights would drain the battery of the vehicle I use for personal needs and for my emergency runs as Chaplain for the Pope County Sheriff's Office. After checking all the fuses under the dash, I knew the problem was obviously deeper than my mechanical/electrical knowledge and proficiency. So, until I could find a solution to the problem, I disconnected a battery cable.

Realizing I could, at any moment, need to drive the Jeep, I went inside to pray about the problem. As I prayed, I was reminded of the words of James, the brother of Jesus, that *"If any of you lacks wisdom, you should ask God, who gives generously to all without finding fault, and it will be given to you"* (James 1:5 NIV).

Having prayed, I went back to my Jeep, opened the driver's door, knelt on the ground and, with the aid of a flashlight, began to examine the wiring between the door and the chassis. As I did this, I was impressed to pull back a rubber boot that covered the wiring. Then I noticed a broken black wire but could not locate both ends of the wire. I then realized that one end of the broken wire was out of my sight and beyond my reach. I felt temporarily discouraged and defeated, then felt strongly impressed to touch the broken black wire to a bolt attaching the door to the chassis. I was amazed to discover that, when the broken wire touched the chassis bolt, the power to the lights was disconnected. The solution was simply to loosen the bolt, attach the wire and retighten the bolt. I then stood to my feet and thanked Abba for wisdom and divine assistance.

Reflection

Dear reader, be encouraged now to know our Heavenly Father is concerned about the smallest details of our lives, and desires to display His love, His compassion, and His provision for us at any time for any need! Trust Him today to lead, to guide and provide! Your problem may be beyond your knowledge, wisdom, or ability to solve, BUT GOD!

FIFTY YEARS OF MIRACLES - EXPERIENCING THE *SUPER*NATURAL

DAY TWENTY-SIX:
THE FLAT TIRE AND THE TROOPER

In 2021 Georgiann and I drove to Dallas, Texas to attend the wedding of a young couple we had connected with in our ministry in Romania. In order to be on time for the wedding on the South side of Dallas, we left Russellville, Arkansas for the six-hour trip, set our cruise control at the posted speed of 75 MPH, and headed toward our destination. Our trip to Dallas would take us West on Interstate 40 into Oklahoma, where we would intersect highway 69-70 toward Dallas. For some unknown reason the route from Oklahoma to the Metro Dallas area seems to be in a perpetual state of construction and/or repair and is often quite a rough ride.

We arrived at our destination in good time before the wedding and had an opportunity to visit with the bride and groom–to-be, and with their parents who had arrived from Romania. The wedding concluded shortly before sundown and, due to our next appointment in Atlanta, Texas, we said our farewells and left immediately.

Traffic on the freeways surrounding Dallas was heavy as usual, with four and five lanes filled with vehicles exceeding the posted speed limits. By the time we intersected Interstate 30 toward Texarkana, it was dark as we sped along at 75 MPH, hoping to reach our destination before 9 PM.

Our trip was going well until we were twenty-five miles East of Dallas, and we heard a popping sound beneath our car, and felt our car swerve to the right edge of the freeway. I stopped as quickly as possible, easing the car to the edge of the pavement just far enough to be safe from the heavy traffic speeding by us.

It was obvious our right rear tire had blown and had to be changed. However, it was also obvious it would be quite hazardous to attempt changing the tire so close to the traffic passing just a few feet from our position. We knew our safest option was to move our car farther from the freeway and obtain road service.

Therefore, I reached into my wallet, pulled out our insurance card, and dialed the number for Road Service. Unfortunately, when Road Service answered, a recorded message informed me that, due to heavy call volume, I should leave my number and receive a call back. I left my number and we waited... and waited... and waited for over an hour. With the 18 wheelers, buses, and automobiles still speeding past us, Georgiann and I prayed for help. I then dialed 911, asked to be connected with the Texas Highway patrol, and requested a Trooper to come to our aid. After waiting another thirty minutes, we saw the blue lights approaching us as the trooper pulled in behind us.

After surveying our situation, the trooper advised me we had to move the car off the shoulder onto a side road where the tire could be safely changed. To accomplish this meant driving the car across a dark ditch and onto the shoulder of the secondary road. The trooper parked his cruiser facing the ditch to provide enough light for us to cross it.

We were in a rural area with no streetlights, so it was obvious changing the tire was going to be a chore. Added to that was the fact that I could not locate the tool needed to operate the hydraulic jack. When it seemed things were going from bad to worse, the trooper said he might have a tool in his cruiser we could use, but due to heavy calls and short staff, he had only a few minutes to spare. Shortly the trooper returned with the tool we needed and proceeded to place the spare and begin raising the car. As I held the flashlight, Georgiann stood near, praying for, and praising the trooper for his act of kindness. Georgiann then said to him, "Sir, you may not realize it, but you are our angel tonight!"

After more than thirty minutes of laboring to raise the car, the tire was finally removed and the spare mounted, and then we saw the damage to the tire. As we examined the tire, we discovered the protruding nail had obviously been there long enough to shred the inside of the tire. I then recognized it was no ordinary nail. It was a roofing nail we picked up when we drove out of the driveway in Russellville, Arkansas earlier that day. We had recently had a new roof installed and, unfortunately, several of the roofing nails had been dropped onto, and not recovered from, the driveway. Consequently, that nail had penetrated our right rear tire, and we had driven several hundred miles at 75 mph heavily congested traffic on a tire being shredded every mile we drove.

As the trooper was preparing to leave, he was astounded we had driven that far without a flat tire and/or an accident. We were able to witness to him of the power of prayer and the watchful care of our Heavenly Father. We then asked if we could pray for him and his own safety. After Georgiann and I prayed for him and his family, I reached into my wallet, took two twenty-dollar bills, and tried to hand them to him. He quickly declined my offer, informing me it was against policy to take the money. I then informed him, the money was not for him, but for his wife!

Before driving away, we thanked him again and Georgiann said, "Sir, you may not realize it, but you are our angel tonight!" And he was! Before we left home, as always, we prayed, not only for divine protection but for divine appointments. Therefore, it was no coincidence the tire lasted until we reached the area where that trooper was working. Further, it was no coincidence I could not reach anyone at Road Service. And finally, it was no coincidence the trooper did not receive one call while spending almost an hour with us!

Abba's angels had protected us, and the Holy Spirit had directed our journey from Arkansas, through Oklahoma, to a divine appointment on the edge of Interstate 30 East of Dallas.

Reflection

The lesson we learned from this experience was the fact that our Heavenly Father orders our steps, guides our path and schedules our appointments. The problems, distractions and delays along our way are often God's way of converting our problems to possibilities and our difficulties into discoveries.

DAY TWENTY-SEVEN:
SERMON FROM ASHES

It was Sunday, January 11, and it was his 32nd birthday celebration. I glanced toward the sound booth in the balcony and welcomed his friendly smile, not realizing this would be the last time Floyd would ever operate the sound board for me.

For months he had followed me like a shadow. He picked my brain for insights into scriptures and ministry. He accompanied me on hospital calls and street ministry. He was a successful businessman yet offered himself as a servant wherever he could be useful.

Floyd's vehicle repossession business had become very successful and one of his dreams was to launch a new business and donate fifty percent of the profits to the church for the first two years, then transfer 100% to the church.

Not only was his life a blessing to his home church, but to other ministries as well. He became a favorite among the counseling staff of Trinity Broadcasting Network, and when it came time to open the new station in Miami, Florida, he flew at his own expense to assist there.

I have never met a man more transparent and honest before God. It was not uncommon for Floyd to come by my office and tearfully admit, "Pastor, I've blown it today...please pray for me!"

At three AM Monday January 11 the ringing telephone beside my bed jolted me to attention. The deputy on the other end said something my mind could not comprehend. I asked him to repeat it, for I thought surely it was a bad dream. But it was a stark reality. I was asked to deliver the message to Floyd's wife that he had been killed in a fiery auto crash on the 405 Freeway.

As the deputy and I drove to the residence, my mind was spinning. Why Floyd? Where was he? What was he doing? I was soon to hear it from his dear wife.

. They left immediately after our Sunday evening service for a birthday party for him at home with all the family. It had been a great, yet tiring day for Floyd. The guys who usually worked with him at night were both sick, so Floyd left home alone at 11:30 PM. Sometime around 1 AM, his pickup rear-ended an 18-wheeler parked on the Southbound shoulder of the San Diego Freeway and Floyd was ushered into the presence of the Lord.

On Monday afternoon, following the accident, a grim search was conducted for any personal effects that could be salvaged from the charred wreckage of his pickup truck. At the scene was one of my deacons (the deputy who escorted me to his home), Floyd's stepson, his business manager, and myself.

We sifted through the ashes carefully, noting that the truck and everything in it was a total loss. We were almost ready to leave the scene when I noticed Floyd's Bible on the right front fender. I stopped in my tracks for I couldn't believe my eyes. The Bible was heavily damaged but was open to a very familiar message from the Apostle Paul to the Philippian believers.

I immediately asked who opened the Bible. The stepson said, "Pastor, I found it that way in the ashes on the floor of the truck cab." I called everyone together and we wept as I read, *"Brothers, I want you to know that what has happened to me has turned out for, rather than against, the advance of the Gospel"* (see Philippians 1:12). As we drove away from the wreckage, I questioned how any good could come out of such tragedy. I was soon to understand!

We scheduled the memorial service for Thursday afternoon. On Tuesday, I received a call from Trinity Broadcasting Network to sing for the Wednesday evening Praise program. As I stood before the cameras on the satellite telecast, I showed the scripture I had taken from the wreckage of Floyd's truck. I reminded the viewers that Floyd had manned the phones just a few feet from where I was standing and had witnessed to many of them about the love of God. As I was sharing, viewers began calling for prayer and surrender to God, and I began to see the fulfillment of the message from the ashes. The program was then replayed and sent to the other outlets throughout the network, and scores called to accept Christ.

Following the telecast, I stood at the pulpit and again shared what we had found in the ashes. At the close of the service, I gave an invitation, and four young business associates came forward, stood by the casket, and surrendered their hearts to the Lord.

Riding to and from the cemetery with the funeral director gave me an opportunity to share the message with him. By the time we were back at our church building, he too was ready. There in the parking lot, with folks all round us, he wept his way through repentance to personal salvation.

Satan may have temporarily rejoiced over the silence of one more witness for Christ. However, he must surely have developed an ulcer over the fact that the sermon from the ashes was preserved and continues to preach and touch lives!

Reflection

Please note I am not suggesting that God was responsible for this accident and heartache, but I am confident of God's word, and promises that *"... we know that in all things God works for the good of those who love him and who have been called according to His purpose"* (Romans 8:28 NIV). I was also reminded of the words of Joseph to his brothers in Genesis 50:20 *"you intended to harm me, but God intended it for good to accomplish what is now being done, the saving of many lives"* (NIV). And finally, the words of the Apostle Paul in Philippians 1:20 *"I eagerly expect and hope that I will in no way be ashamed, but will have sufficient courage so that now as always Christ will be exalted in my body, whether by life or be death"* (NIV).

Whatever you are facing today, whatever tragedies or crises have come your way, stand on the promises of our Heavenly Father, and expect Him to turn tragedy into triumph for your good and His Glory!

DAY TWENTY-EIGHT:
THE KILLER TORNADO

The following article appeared in the New York Times, June 6, 1974:

8 Reported Killed by Tornado in Arkansas Town

FORREST CITY, Ark., June 6

"A tornado tore through sections of this eastern Arkansas town tonight, and a deputy sheriff said eight persons had been killed. At least 200 persons were reported injured.

Joe McCollum, deputy sheriff in the town of 12,500, said all the dead had been trapped in a large discount store that was demolished. He said about 75 persons were injured when the roof of the Gibbon's discount store collapsed."

Georgiann and I were there lying in a drainage ditch approximately a hundred yards from the store entrance.

While serving as Youth and Music Ministers at First Assembly of God in Russellville Arkansas in the early Seventies, Georgiann and I were selected to serve as judges for the Regional Teen Talent/Bible Quiz competition in Memphis, Tennessee. A couple in our church, volunteered to watch our sons, Chris and Steve while we were in Memphis. Chris was three and Steve was two at the time.

On the morning of June 6, we dropped the boys at the home of our friends and headed East on Interstate 40, planning to arrive in Memphis early enough to check in to our hotel and have dinner before the meeting that night. However, things would not go as planned for this three-hour drive. As we left Little Rock, heading toward Memphis, we began to notice dark intimidating clouds forming, threatening to bring heavy rain to our area. Tuning our car radio to a Little Rock channel, we heard the warnings of severe thunderstorms along I40, so we planned to hurry and try to stay ahead of the East bound storms.

However, approximately two hours into our trip, the clouds became darker, and we began to encounter very heavy rain and strong winds.

As we approached Forrest City, the rain was so heavy, the water on the freeway was so deep it was obviously becoming dangerous to keep our 69 Buick Riviera from hydroplaning, so I started looking for the nearest exit. Approximately a mile down the road, I pulled off the freeway and stopped at a gas station that had a phone booth I could use to call ahead to inform our friends in Memphis we would be late arriving.

As soon as I stopped the car, Georgiann headed inside the station to use the restroom and I headed for the phone booth. As I inserted my coins and dialed the phone to reach our friends in Memphis, heavy thunder began to rumble, and the winds became very strong. Then, as I looked West through the phone booth, I saw two large funnel clouds approaching, heading straight toward us. Growing up near the Arkansas/Texas border I had been near numerous severe storms, but never had I been in the direct path of not, just one, but two twisters! I quickly slammed down the receiver and ran into the gas station, yelling for Georgiann to get out.

As Georgiann ran out of the station to meet me, the two funnel clouds formed one huge funnel half a block wide and was heading straight toward the gas station. I grabbed Georgiann's hand, and we ran to a wide drainage ditch on the East side of the station. Sliding down the embankment, we would hear the angry storm approaching with the sound of a rumbling train.

As soon as we hit the bottom of the ditch, another couple slid in right behind us. This couple, from a Northern State, had been sitting in their vehicle, terrified of the approaching storm, not knowing what to do. But, when they saw us head for the ditch, they followed us.

As the storm got closer and the ground began to shake, I wrapped my arms around Georgiann and my legs around a small sapling growing in the ditch, and we began to pray. Knowing the ditch was wide and we could be sucked out of it or be crushed by debris blown into it, the thought of leaving our two little boys as orphans crossed our minds, and we cried out to God to turn the storm.

As we buried our faces in the mud, the storm drew closer, the ground shook furiously, and it sounded as if a freight train would pass directly over us. A time or two I turned my head enough to see large items and debris flying overhead. What was mere moments seemed like an eternity as we clung to each other and cried out to God for protection.

When the rumbling and shaking stopped we crawled out of the ditch and the sight was horrible. Some of the vehicles parked on the South side of the freeway had been carried across to the Northern side and piled up like a salvage yard. Miraculously, our car had been spared, but sandblasted. As we surveyed the damage around us, it was hard to believe our eyes. The gas station had lost its roof but was still standing. Apparently, the tornado had turned North as it approached the gas station and leveled a shopping center a hundred yards from us. The Gibsons Discount center was now just a few feet high and completely demolished. Knowing people were trapped under the debris I left Georgiann with our car and began running through the water toward the collapsed building.

As I approached, I could hear screaming, crying, and moaning. Doing my best to avoid downed power lines, I crawled under the roof of the building, not more than four feet high, and made my way toward the moaning sounds. A few feet into the debris, I located a woman trapped under a steel beam. She was obviously seriously injured and frightened, so I began to speak to her and pray with and for her, assuring her that help was on the way. I stayed with her until a rescue team arrived to free and transport her to a hospital. Due to the horrendous damage to the building, the lady was the only person I could reach. Other rescue teams were arriving and assisting, and we formed a relay team passing the injured one to another until they could be loaded into ambulances. I then waded back across the flooded parking lot to Georgiann. Georgiann was wearing a brand-new full-length dress and I was in a suit. We were both soaked, and I was covered with mud and blood from the rescue efforts.

Before getting into our car, I examined it for damage. Although we had no broken glass, it was obvious we would need a new paint job, but we were so grateful for our Father's protection. We sat for several minutes, stunned by the destruction around us. We joined hands and thanked Abba for sparing our lives, then drove across the freeway to a Holiday Inn where we could phone ahead to notify our friends waiting for us in Memphis.

We were both still shaken as we checked into our motel in Memphis. As we unloaded our luggage and headed for our room, we could hear the heavy thunder and could see the dark clouds approaching from the West. We quickly moved into our room and turned on the TV set, just in time to see and hear the warnings of a tornado approaching. Following storm protocol, we instantly grabbed blankets from the beds to cover ourselves and ran into the bathroom where Georgiann crawled into the bathtub.

We would not know till later that eight people had perished under the collapsed shopping center. Obviously, I never knew the name of the injured lady I prayed with, nor did I know if she survived. However, I do know that a supernatural power was at work that day. Georgiann and I could have died in the storm, but we were spared. I was able to cross the parking lot and get far enough under the rubble to be at the side of that precious wife and mother, and we were permitted to raise our two sons, plus a beautiful daughter to become Christ-following world changers.

As we looked back on that frightening experience, several facts became obvious to us:

Had we not parked the car where we did, it would have likely been demolished; Had the other couple not seen us run for the ditch and followed us they could have been seriously injured or killed by the flying debris; and had I not been able to cross the flooded parking lot, I could not have prayed with the injured lady and assisted the rescue teams with the other victims. And, had the storm passed directly over the ditch, motor vehicles could have easily been tossed in on us.

Reflection

In Psalm 46:1-3 (NIV), the Psalmist gave us a powerful promise concerning our Father, *"1 **God is our refuge and strength, a very present help in trouble**. 2 Therefore will not we fear, though the earth be removed, and though the mountains be carried into the midst of the sea; 3 Though the waters thereof roar and be troubled, though the mountains shake with the swelling thereof. Selah."*

Stop right now and thank our Father for the many times He has protected you and yours from harm, then thank Him in advance for His watchful care tomorrow and the coming days!

DAY TWENTY-NINE:
SPIRITUAL VISITATION AT
PHANTOM OF THE OPERA

Back in the mid-Nineties, Georgiann and I attended a pastor's conference on the Northern side of London, England. Not only were we blessed by the powerful messages and the praise and worship sessions at the conference, but the prophetic words delivered were very encouraging. Toward the end of the conference a prophetic message was given that the Holy Spirit was going to move into every facet of society, and God's *Ekklesia* would pervade all seven mountains of society.

I found that prophetic message to be very exciting, because back in In 1975, Bill Bright, founder of Campus Crusade and Loren Cunningham, founder of Youth With a Mission (YWAM), developed a God-given, world-changing strategy. Their mandate: Bring Godly change to a nation by reaching its seven spheres, or mountains, of societal influence.

They concluded that in order to truly transform any nation with the Gospel of Jesus Christ, these seven facets of society must be reached: Religion, Family, Education, Government, Media, Arts & Entertainment, and Business. Georgiann and I left the conference blessed and encouraged at what we had heard and experienced. However, the Holy Spirit was not finished speaking to us!

Following the conference, we had a couple days to spend in London, so I purchased tickets to *The Phantom of the Opera* in downtown London. We had only seen the production on film, so we were thrilled at the idea of seeing a live production by some of the world's greatest vocalists and actors.

We arrived at the theater early and were thrilled to discover our seats were in the mid-center section near the stage. As the production began, we were captivated by the incredible talent of these world-renowned performers.

However, about halfway through the show something very strange occurred. As one of the singers was delivering a powerful presentation, I suddenly began to tremble and weep uncontrollably. In fact, my body was shaking so hard, I was afraid I would cause a disturbance, but the lighting was so dim in the auditorium only Georgiann was aware and amazed at the scene.

At that moment, I felt the power of the Holy Spirit moving upon my emotions and my body in a measure I had never experienced, and I began to pray silently, asking God what and why? In fact, I said to Him, "Why am I weeping? Why do I feel such a powerful anointing here? This is a theater not a church!"

Then, I heard him speak to my spirit, "But, my church is here!" He then said to me, "Look around you. What do you see here and what are you experiencing? I replied, "I see a thousand people captured and captivated by the talent on display here. People are on the edge of their seats, almost spell bound by the absolute precision, control, and beauty of the voices on this stage!"

Then, He spoke to me, "Yes, and I'm taking it ALL back! I'm taking back the Arts and Entertainment, Religion, Family, Education, Government, Media, and Business. There is coming a time in the near future when men and women will write, sing, and perform, not with mere human talent, but under the anointing of the Holy Spirit, and thousands will feel what you feel here! Thousands will experience the presence of God and come to know Him and Lord and Savior!"

We boarded our flight the next day, still amazed and shaken by what we had heard at the conference and experienced in the theater. I returned to my pastoral duties here in Arkansas with a renewed passion for the presence of the Holy Spirit and began to pray for the fulfilment of what I had heard, and I wondered when we would see it come to pass. Then, in 1994 born-again Christian Roma Downey, president of Lightworkers Media, the faith and family division of MGM, launched the series called *Touched by an Angel.* In addition, Roma and her husband, Mark Burnett, produced the Emmy-nominated miniseries *THE BIBLE* for the History channel. The Bible was watched by over

100 million people in the United States. They went on to produce many other faith-based films, including *Ben-Hur, Son of God, Resurrection, Messiah and Country Ever After.*

THEN in 2004 Actor, Mel Gibson produced and released one of the most powerful films ever released. *The Passion of the Christ* made $612 million globally at the box office on its $30 million budget, making it the highest grossing R-rated film in US cinemas. In spite of the fact, Hollywood was reluctant to finance the film, Mel Gibson felt strongly enough about this to put his own money behind it. And, obviously, the Holy Spirit was the Chief Director of this powerful Gospel presentation.

Then, in 2019 Dallas Jenkins produced the first multi-season series about the life of Christ and the highest crowd-funded TV series or film project of all time.

The Chosen portrays Jesus through the eyes of those who met Him and is literally changing lives around the world. *The Chosen* is the first movie series of its kind, financed by Christian believers around the world, who, after watching an episode, pay it forward for others to view it.

According to IBL New York, Angel Studios, the streaming platform behind the Christian series *The Chosen,* announced this week (January 8) it had raised $47 million in funding from venture capitalists. The financing was led by VC firm Gigafund and Bain-backed Uncorrelated Venture. Original seed investors Alta Ventures and Kickstart Fund also participated.

In addition to VC money, $5 million was crowdsourced directly from fans.

Angel Studios presented the financing injection as an effort *"to bring control of the entertainment industry back to consumers and creators"* and *"give Hollywood a remake."*

"The round caps off a major comeback year for cofounders Neal and Jeffrey Harmon, who led Angel Studios to over $100 million in annual revenue just one year after Disney and Warner Bros tried to shut the studio down in court," said the company. CAN I GET A PRAISE GOD?!

Not only is Almighty God moving in the Arts and Entertainment field but also the other six mountains are being shaken as born-again believers are recognizing they have been chosen, ordained, and anointed to find their place and their purpose here on Earth.

In 2000, when my first book *Stop **Going** To Church...The Dynamics Of **Being** The Church* was published, I had no idea what would happen over the next twenty years as prominent Church leaders began to stress the importance of the *Ekklesia* moving outside our buildings to invade, infect and influence every facet of society.

One of the first to make a major transition was Francis Chan, the former teaching pastor of Cornerstone Community Church, an Evangelical church in Simi Valley, California. When Francis realized that he had become a celebrity pastor of a Mega-church, he was so convicted by the Holy Spirit he resigned his position and moved back to Hong Kong where he is leading believers to present the Kingdom of God to every facet of their societies.

Then in Lubbock, Texas, Chris Gallanos, pastor of a ten-thousand-member Mega Church, was challenged by the Holy Spirit to move his congregation into homes in order to influence their neighbors with the love and message of Christ. Chris' book, *From Megachurch To Multiplication*, is rocking the American church with an explosive message reminding us of the meaning, message, and method of the *Ekklesia*.

Finally, right here at home, our church experienced a major transition in 2020. In 1990 we launched a new work, called Life Center Church, in Russellville, Arkansas, with the expressed mission of reaching the unreached, unchurched unbeliever in our area. Within ten years our congregation had grown to 500, but I sensed we had regressed to a normal, healthy, happy group of believers and I was once again challenged with the Biblical meaning, message, and methodology of the Church, and I came to realize the majority of our church growth was members transferring from other congregations.

Therefore, in 2002, I resigned my position, and Steve Pyle, our youngest son, became the lead pastor, with a renewed focus on reaching the unchurched, de-churched, unbelievers of our area. Not long after that transition, we changed the name of our church to The Journey and within the next ten years we had expanded to three campuses with over 1500 in weekly attendance.

Then, shortly before the Covid pandemic, Steve felt the need to challenge the congregation to reach their neighbors and planned to move toward home groups meeting at least monthly. When the Covid pandemic hit and shutdowns were mandated, our church moved into our homes and started loving our neighbors, and we never returned to "normal" meetings. By the way, in our last baptismal service four out of the seven baptized were converted in our homes.

In fact, so convinced were we that our congregation was called to invade and engage our neighborhoods that we transferred our largest building to one of our other outreach ministries that converted the building to house many different ministries, including:

- A fully equipped state of the art free medical clinic, where our area physicians and area pastors rotate, giving of their time to serve those in need
- Food 4 Children (serving up to 20,000 meals per week to needy children in our area)
- The Pope County 100 Families project, moving 100 families from Crisis to Career
- ARVAC housing
- A fully equipped garage and fulltime mechanic (who came through our homeless ministry), to repair the vehicles donated to our ministries for needy families

Due to the dramatic shift in our methodology of doing church, it appears we are now reaching more with the message of the Kingdom of God than all our previous years. Oh, by the way, as of January 1 of 2023, we have a new mayor in our city. He is Fred Teague, one of our church elders and the founder and director of The Russ Bus, one of the largest and most effective homeless ministries in the State of Arkansas.

It is evident our Heavenly Father, CEO of the universe, has moved out of our buildings into the marketplace and His Ekklesia is transforming all seven mountains by His Will, His love, and His power!

Reflection

My prayer for each reader is that you have found your calling and purpose and are being salt and light wherever you have been placed to advance the Kingdom of God.

Will you take a few moments today to ask Abba God why you are at this place and time? Read His Word expecting Him to guide and direct you. Then, listen to His prompting, walk out your door today, expecting divine encounters and opportunities to change your world with His love, His compassion, His wisdom, and power!

DAY THIRTY:
THE SUPERNATURAL POWER OF PRAYER

Following our trip to London and the Phantom of the Opera supernatural experience in the mid-nineties, Georgiann and I boarded our flight from London Heathrow to Atlanta, Georgia.

Several hours into our flight, I had another supernatural encounter with the Holy Spirit, and began to tremble and weep uncontrollably. As this was happening to me, Georgiann returned to our row from the restroom and needed to get past me to her seat. However, I could not move! It was as if my feet were glued to the floor or were so heavy, I couldn't move them. I later recalled that the Hebrew definition for "Glory" is heaviness or weight, signifying the ideas of importance, greatness, honour, splendor, power, and so on. The glory of God had fallen on me and I was literally weighed down by His presence!

Due to the fact I could not move my feet or legs, Georgiann had to crawl over me to get to her seat. Slipping over me and into her seat, Georgiann asked, "What is happening to you?" I replied, "I don't know. I just know the Holy Spirit has overwhelmed me!" She replied, "I know, I felt it in the restroom!"

As I sat beside Georgiann shaking and weeping, I began to ask the Father to show me "Why here, why now?" It was still dark in the plane, but I could see the panel above us that displayed our altitude at 39,500 feet and our speed at 580 miles per hour. I saw nothing spiritual about that. Then, I felt impressed to check the time. As I pressed the button on the side of my wristwatch, I noted it was 5:20 AM London time. I then pressed our time in Arkansas and noticed it was 11:20 AM.

THEN, it dawned on me, our church family at Life Center Church in Russellville, Arkansas, was standing and worshiping.

They knew Georgiann and I were enroute home, and someone was praying for us. And, although we were separated by several thousand miles, as they stood, worshiping, and praying we connected in the Supernatural realm. In Russellville, Arkansas, our friends reached up and touched God on our behalf, and halfway around the world, the Holy Spirit reached down and surrounded us with His awesome, glorious presence.

Reflection

Please recognize that prayer is so much more than reciting words of petition to our Heavenly Father. It is actually humanity tapping into divinity...the natural connecting with the Supernatural!

Whatever you are facing today, recognize you are not limited to your physical or intellectual abilities, but as a believer, the same Spirit that raised Christ from the dead now lives in you! (Romans 6:10-11)

AND, in addition to that reality, know that "you are of God *and* you belong to Him and have [already] overcome them [the agents of the antichrist]; because He who is in you is greater than he (Satan) who is in the world [of sinful mankind]" (1 John 4:4 AMP). Therefore, whatever your challenge today, rejoice in the fact that you, plus God equal a majority! Know that, through the power of prayer, you can reach across your city, your state, your nation or around the world and touch someone with the supernatural power of the Holy Spirit! Do it right now and expect good reports!

AN INVITATION

If you, dear reader, have not accepted Christ as your personal Lord and savior, I invite you to do so at this point, so I point you to what is known as "The Roman Road": Romans 323 tells us that "all have sinned and fallen short of the glory of God, and the wages of sin is death." And Romans 6: 23 tells us "That the wages of sin is death." That's the bad news!

The good news is found in the final portion of Romans 3: 23, "but the gift of God is eternal life through Christ Jesus our Lord." Then Romans 10: 9-10 tells us, "If you declare with your mouth, 'Jesus is Lord,' and believe in your heart that God raised him from the dead, you will be saved. For it is with your heart that you believe and are justified, and it is with your mouth that you profess your faith and are saved."

Jesus, the Christ, came to earth and gave His life to redeem us from the control of Satan. If this is a need in your life, call on him now...he is waiting and ready to hear from you, forgive you and give you eternal life. If you have prayed this prayer and responded to and received the gift of salvation, welcome to the family and let me hear from you!

SUMMARY

I was ready to type "Conclusion" when I was reminded this story is far from over, and as long as I am in this earth suit, Abba will continue to reveal his power, perform his miracles and send his ministering angels to assist us on our journey Home. Therefore, let me encourage each reader to place your trust in the One who loves you more than you can imagine and wants to reveal His plan and provision for your daily life. In the days to come I would love to hear from you as you witness Divine interventions and provisions along the way! You can connect with me on Facebook or e-mail: larrypfs@gmail.com.

ENDORSEMENTS

This is a book everyone who knows Christ should read. You will laugh at one episode and then cry at the next. In all of these delightful stories you will marvel at the goodness of God.

I especially loved The Toddler in the Street because I know Steve, now a strong leader of his own powerful ministry. Thank God for the long pants and sleeves! I also warmed to Thousand-Fold Return. How good is God to multiply and return a harvest from a seed when we sacrifice to help someone else in need.

As I would expect, the book is well-written. It's hard to put down. One story a day from this book will keep you in victory all day!

Dr. Ron Cottle

President, REC Ministries

Embassy College

Larry Pyle's book recounting stories of actual miracles he and Georgiann have experienced will inspire and encourage you to believe God for answers to your prayers, even when answers seem impossible.

With societal cynicism so pervasive and doubters prevalent, many have concluded that testimonies of the miraculous are untrue and miracles non-existent. Because of my long-standing friendship with the author, I am convinced every fact in every story is absolutely true.

Your faith will be strengthened as each miracle story reminds you that God's past performance predicts His future behavior.

Alton Garrison

Acts 2 Journey

Executive Director

Dr. Larry Pyle's Fifty Years of Miracles book represents the practical and potential walk of the true church of Jesus Christ on the earth. Here, I'm certifying each of Larry's wondrous stories as not coincidental, but real living encounters by divine appointment. However, what we call on earth miracles, in God's Kingdom, are called the nature of God, and it should become every believer's norm.

While reading this book, I was reminded of Larry's wide joyful smile and tearful eyes while speaking the word of God in our pastoral Bible seminars in Romania. All our pastors regardless of their confessions and backgrounds loved him as the man who was sent by Jesus himself to guide and teach us how to walk daily with Jesus. Larry is a true apostle of Jesus Christ who should be honored and believed for any uttered oracles from God.

Pastor John Dolinschi

Founder and President of Christ Commission for Romania

Pastoral Fellowship Europe-America

OTHER BOOKS BY LARRY PYLE

"Stop *GOING* to church! (The dynamics of *BEING* the Church)"

- Available on Amazon and Kindle

"Keeping the Church Relevant... by Breaking the Cycle of Redundancy"

- Available on Amazon and Kindle

ABOUT THE AUTHOR

Larry Pyle is founder and President of Successful Living Concepts, Inc. He holds a Doctorate of Ministry and has been in active church ministry since 1971.

He and his wife, Georgiann have served churches across America, Canada, and Eastern Europe.

Larry is the founder of Life Center Church (now the Journey) in Russellville, Arkansas, and serves on the oversight teams for churches in Arkansas, Texas, Chicago, Indiana, and Florida.

In addition to serving as a Church Growth and Financial Consultant to churches across America, Larry has served as the Bishop to Romania for the Acts Network (Apostolic Council of Transformational Servant-Leaders).

Made in the USA
Coppell, TX
23 June 2023

18437955R00102